THE DRAGON AND THE CROSS:
WHY EUROPEAN CHRISTIANITY FAILED TO TAKE ROOT IN CHINA

By

Louis K. Ho
DMin, MDiv, MTS, MEd. MLS

St. Stephen's Theological College
At the University of Alberta
Edmonton, Canada

May 1st, 2009

Copyright © 2009
by Louis K. Ho DMin, MDiv, MTS, MEd. MLS

THE DRAGON AND THE CROSS
by Louis K. Ho DMin, MDiv, MTS, MEd. MLS

Printed in the United States of America

ISBN 978-1-60791-259-0
Library of Congress Cataloging-in-Publication Data

All rights reserved solely by the author. The author guarantees all contents are original and do not infringe upon the legal rights of any other person or work. No part of this book may be reproduced in any form without the permission of the author. The views expressed in this book are not necessarily those of the publisher.

Unless otherwise indicated, Bible quotations are taken from the New International Version. Copyright © 1984 by International Bible Society.

Ho, Louis Kamtat, 1935-
The Dragon and the Cross:
Why European Christianity Failed to Take Root in China/Louis K. Ho
p. cm Includes bibliographical references
1. Christianity — China
2. Christianity and Politics — China — 1949-2009
3. Ricci, Matteo, 1552-1610 — Italian Missionary to China
4. China — Church History
5. Missions — China - History
I. Title
BR 1285
275.1

www.xulonpress.com

To Edward & Anne

Shalom:
Peace be with you.

Laura

July 2010

CONTENTS

Acknowledgement xi
Map of China xiii
Photo: Bibles printed and bound at Amity Printing Press in
    China..xv
Romanization of Written Chinese Characters................. xvii
Preface.. xix
    Rationale for This Book... xix
    Information Source (Research Methodology) xix
    Chapter Outline..xx
    Limitations xxiii

PART ONE: HISTORICAL AND CONTEMPORARY
ISSUES OF CHRISTIANITY IN CHINA...................25

Chapter I: INTRODUCTION 27
    Contemporary China..27
    Political and Economic Perspective..............................29
    Economic Growth 30
    Moral Vacuum..32
    The Role of Christianity in Contemporary Chinese
        Society..34
    A Popular Religion...35
    European Christianity 36
    Failure of European Christianity to Inculturate
        in China..37
    End Notes..39

v

Chapter II: A HISTORICAL PERSPECTIVE OF CHINA WITH PARTICULAR EMPHASIS ON THE 16TH AND 17TH CENTURY DURING THE EUROPEAN RENAISSANCE......41
Timeline of Major History of China......43
The Ming Dynasty......44
The Manchu or Qing (Ch'ing) Dynasty......47
End Notes......51
Chapter III: CONFUCIUS' MORAL TEACHING AND ITS RELATIONSHIP TO CHRISTIANITY......53
Biographic Background......53
Confucius' Moral Teaching......56
Confucianism and Christianity......59
End Notes......62
Chapter IV: A HISTORICAL PERSPECTIVE OF CHRISTIANITY IN CHINA......63
End Notes......66
Chapter V: INCULTURATION......67
St. Francis Xavier......69
Christianity as Institutionalized Religion in China......72
The Christian Church, Cultural Accommodation and Political Harmonization......72
End Notes......76
Chapter VI: EPISODES OF THE FAILURE OF EUROPEAN CHRISTIANITY TO TAKE ROOT IN CHINA......79
86AD to 1500 AD......79
Christianity Under the Jesuit Policy of Accommodation 1583-1742......82
The Problem of Ancestor Worship......82
Christianity Followed the Steps of Western Imperialism 1842-1949......86
Protestant Evangelism......87
Christianity at the Brink of Being Wiped Out......90
End Notes......93

Chapter VII: THE DEVELOPMENT OF AN
   INDIGENOUS CHURCH SINCE 1978......................95
   The Roman Catholic Church 96
   The Underground Catholic Church............................99
   The Protestant Church..101
   The Protestant House Church 102
   End Notes..106
Chapter VIII: THE CURRENT RELIGIOUS POLICY OF
   CHINA RELATING TO CHRISTIANITY 107
   The Religious Policy of Deng Xiao-Ping 110
   Factors favoring Religious Development 111
   Relationship Between Ideological Control and
      Religious Development..112
   Document 19 and the Religious Clause of the Chinese
      Constitution..113
   Method of Religious Control 120
   Orthodoxy of Christian Teaching in China................122
   End Notes..126
Chapter IX: WILL CHRSITIANITY EVER TAKE ROOT
   IN CHINA?...129
   Christianity as Institutionalized Religion in China....132
   The Future of the Catholic Church in China..............133
   The Future of the Protestant Church in China 140
   Protestantism and Catholicism Compared..................142
   Political Harmonization 144
   Conclusion: The Church with a Vision......................145
   End Notes..148
Part One Bibliography 151

PART TWO: CASE STUDY OF CULTURAL
   ACCOMMODTION: MATTEO RICCI AND THE
   JESUIT MISSION IN CHINA 1583-1742 161

THE DRAGON AND THE CROSS

Episode One: WESTERN EUROPE DURING THE
RENAISSANCE AND THE AGE OF
DISCOVERY 163
Geographic Exploration and Discoveries 163
The Reformation 165
The European Renaissance 167
End Notes 168

Episode Two: BIOGRAPHICAL BACKGROUND OF
MATTEO RICCI 169
400th Anniversary of the Arrival of Matteo Ricci in
China 169
Biographical Sketch 171
Arrival in Macao 173
Arrival in China 174
Putting Accommodation Theories into Practice 175
Episode Three: RICCI'S METHOD OF HARMONIZAING
CONFUCIANISM WITH CHRISTIANITY 185
End Notes 191
Episode Four: CHRISTIANITY MEETS
CONFUCIANISM 193
God the Creator 194
Life after Death 197
The Concept of Morality 198
The Problem of Ancestral Worship 201
End Notes 204
Episode Five: THE RESPONSE FROM ROME 207
Apostolic Legations to China 210
Conclusion of the Rites Issue 213
End Notes 215
Episode Six: PERSECUTION 217
Emperor K'ang His 218
The First Imperial Audience 220
The Second Imperial Audience 223

The Persecution of Chinese Christians 224
End Notes 226
Episode Seven: CONCLUSION: THE LEGACY OF
   MATTEO RICCI AND THE JESUIT MISSION 227
   Jesuit Impact on Christianizing China 228
   Other Contributions 229
   The Relevance of Ricci 231
Part Two Bibliography 235

Appendix: The Pope's Pastoral Letter to the Catholic
   Church in China, May 2007 239

ACKNOWLEDGEMENT

I would never have been able to realize the publication of this book without the encouragement, advice, guidance, support and assistance of the following people. I would like to use this opportunity to express my sincerest gratitude and thanks to all of them.

Rev. Dr. Martin Moser, omi, for his inspiration and guidance in completing my doctoral dissertation which has formed the basis of this work;

Father. Hal Dallmann, Vicar of St. Barnabas Anglican Church in Edmonton, for proofreading of the manuscript;

The Most Rev. Dr. Sean E. Larkin, Archbishop, Province II (Europe & Canada), UAD; Dr. Earle Sharam, Dean of St. Stephen's Theological College; and Father Hal Dallmann, Vicar of St. Barnabas, for their advance acclaim and personal comments on this work for the blurb of the book cover;

My good friend Margaret Keene for her insightful suggestion of the book title;

My family: Kimmy, Francis, Christopher and Catherine for encouraging and sustaining me to finish the manuscript;

And all my valued friends who have inspired and encouraged me in my journey to realize this publication.

Thank you all indeed, and may the Good Lord bless you for your generous assistance in making this book a reality.

Louis K. Ho, D. Min.
St. Stephen's Theological College
Edmonton, Canada
May 1st, 2009

Map of China

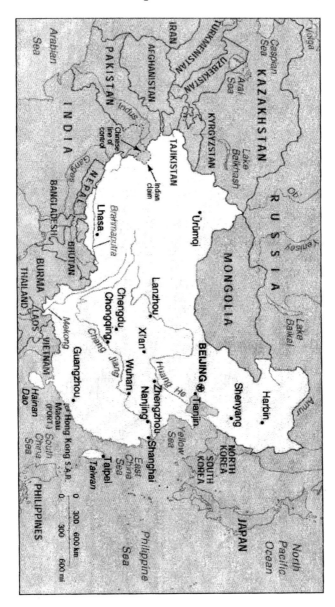

Photo: Bibles printed and bound at Amity Printing Press
in Nanjing, China.
Used by permission of the Canadian Bible Society

"Amity Press has printed over 46 million Bibles in the past 20 years! Just 40 years ago the Bible was banned to China – today it's one of the best selling books."

ROMANIZATION OF CHINESE WRITTEN CHARACTERS

1. Although spoken Chinese has different forms according to geographical regions (the most common ones are Mandarin and Cantonese), the written Chinese language has two basic forms: (a) the traditional (complicated) form mainly used by Chinese in Hong Kong, Macao, Taiwan and Overseas, and (b) the simplified form used by the government and the people in mainland China.

2. Romanization of the Chinese characters using the Roman (Latin) alphabets was initially developed by two English diplomat-scholars: Sir Thomas Wade during the 1800's and Herbert A. Giles during the 1900's. This system is known as the Wade-Giles System. It was a popular system to Romanize Chinese written characters during the 19th Century and the first half of the Twentieth Century.

3. In 1950, the new Communist government in China introduced a new system to standardize the Romanization of the Chinese written characters. It is known as the Pinyin system, and the Government used it in all news reports for, and in all communications with, foreigners who do not comprehend the Chinese written characters. Since 1978 Pinyin has become the official way of Romanizing

Chinese written characters both inside and outside China.

4. The following is a comparison of the two systems. (a) Wade-Giles: Mao Tse-tung; Tang Hsiao-p'ing. (b) Pinyin: Mao Zedong; Deng Xiaoping.

5. Historical research employed in this research involves earlier literature on China before 1979, and they commonly used the Wade-Giles System. Recent literature on Chinese Studies, however, has followed the official Pinyin System for romanizing the written Chinese characters. Hence, both the Wade-Giles and Pinyin Systems are used in this research, either separately or together. Chinese written characters are given whenever possible to help overcome the possible confusion of the two systems.

PREFACE

Rationale

In their visits to China people are generally surprised to see that both Protestant and Catholic churches are well attended on Sundays. Many thought that Christianity had vanished in China under previous persecutions. Those who are interested in contemporary China often have two questions in mind. The first is: Did Christianity fail to take root in China? And the second question is: Will Christianity take root in China? To answer these questions I have attempted to put this book together.

Information Source (Research Methodology)

This book is the culmination of my studies for the Doctor of Ministry degree and years of post-doctoral research and personal reflection. For methodology I have used both the historical and qualitative methods of research. The historical research involved mainly literature review of both the cultural and missionary history of China in order to gain an insight into the past. For the qualitative method of research on contemporary China I have travelled extensively over the country. It is largely an investigative process whereby I immersed myself in the situation in order to make sense of the phenomenon by observing and interviewing people in my visits. The data so collected were later contrasted, compared, replicated, catalogued and classified. In this process, as the research entered the subjects' or informants' world and through ongoing interaction, I sought the informants' perspectives and meanings to arrive at an understanding of the present situation of Christianity in China today.

China is a huge country both by size and population. Geographically, China can be divided into three broad regions with dense population – the Yellow River Plain in the north, the Yangtze Plain in the centre and the Pearl River Plain in the south. Two population centers were selected for each region based on accessibility and the history of the Christianity there. Hong Kong served as a base for the travel. For confidentiality and personal security I am unable to reveal the travel details.

I have my cultural roots in China and can relate well to the church situation there. Born in Macao and raised in Hong Kong, I have been in and out of China many times in my life. Being of Chinese ethnic origin I can communicate well with the people. As an Adjunct Faculty Member of St. Stephen's Theological College on the campus of the University of Alberta in Canada, I have the connections and the help I need to gather the information and the data for this study. I also have the cultural sensitivity to look beyond the surface of events to obtain the insight for this research. Since coming to Canada in 1968, as a committed Christian I have become involved in the activities of both the Catholic and Protestant denominations, and have come to recognize both the strengths and weaknesses of them both.

Chapter Outline

As an introduction, Chapter 1, in a nutshell, describes the peaceful emergence of China as a world power, and narrates the political and social problems confronting China today. In view of these vast problems, and in order to achieve social stability, the government of China has resorted to strict social control. Civil liberty is limited there. Leaders in China have made it clear that unless there is social stability, China's economic reform will not be able to continue at the present speed. The leadership has applied the same social control on religion. It is necessary for us to understand China's policy of social control before we can successfully plant Christianity in China for it to take root.

Chapter II gives a historical perspective of China in the 16th and 17th centuries for us to understand the conditions there when Christian evangelization of China intensified. Chapter III provides, in a nutshell, the moral teaching of Confucius which has dominated Chinese society for more than two thousand years. This will help us understand how Christian evangelism in the 17th Century was able to harmonize with this cultural force.

Chapter IV gives a brief history of Christianity in China during different phases. The earliest contact of Christianity (Nestorianism) with the Chinese culture, according to the popular notion, began in 635 C.E. and ended in the early part of 1300s. (1) During this phase Christianity was unable to take root in China as it made no effort to inculturate. As Buddhism was influential during this historical period, some Nestorian temples were even converted into local temples. The second phase began in 1294 during the Yuen Dynasty when Catholic Franciscan missionaries came to China and Nestorianism began to fade out. Again, this phase did not last very long as Europe was in a chaotic and unsettled time. The third phase of Christian history in China began when Jesuit Matteo Ricci arrived in China in 1583. His policy of theological accommodation won him the respect of the Chinese people. Unfortunately the Rites Controversy with Rome took away all his effort, and the church came under Chinese persecution in 1705. Since then for almost two hundred years, Christianity was totally wiped out of China until 1842, when Britain in the infamous Opium War defeated China. This began the fourth phase of the history of Christianity in China when Christianity became part of imperialism and colonialism. The Communist takeover of China in 1949 began the fifth phase of history of Christianity in China, when the new government persecuted the Church. The death of Mao Zedong started a new era for Christianity in China. This is the sixth and the current phase. Christianity germinated from the ashes and has started to bloom, particularly in the Protestant Church.

Chapter V explains the concept of inculturation in evangelism and introduces the Jesuit method of accommodation. As well, it also discusses the implication of inculturation for present day evangelism in China. Chapter VI analyzes the historical failure of Christianity to take root in China from various aspects such as cultural, societal, theological, liturgical, and political. Chapter VII discusses the development of an indigenous Christian Church taking root in contemporary China and a comparative evaluation of the Catholic and Protestant Churches in their attempt to take root in Chinese soil. Chapter VIII contains an important chapter on the religious policy of contemporary China, and is a must read for anyone who is concerned about the future of the Christian Church in China. Chapter XI gives a personal perspective of the future of Christianity to firmly take root in Chinese soil.

Part II is a case study concerning the inculturation method of Matteo Ricci and the Jesuit Mission in China from 1583-1742 C.E. It is an important episode of Christian missionary history. Part III is an appendix containing the Pope's Pastoral Letter in May 2007 to the Catholic Church in China. This letter is lengthy but it unveils the official policy of the Holy See (Vatican) for the Chinese Church, and is important for anyone who is concerned about Sino-Vatican Relations.

Limitations

As much as I want to remain focused in my research, I am therefore fully aware of my limitations. Our interpretation of information cannot be completely unbiased, because we are influenced by our background and value judgments. Contemporary social sciences researcher Sandra Kirby has consoled us by pointing out that "there is no such thing as an impartial or unimpassioned researcher...Rather than consider your interests as limitations of your vision, consider them as enhancements of your vision, built on the diversity of your experience. As we explore ideas, a single piece of research often produces more than one equally plausible conclusion. Rather than debate which is more correct, we believe that it is the diversity of the creators of knowledge that accounts for the diversity of research and understanding about human life that exists." (2)

If I have offended any reader in my personal observation of the church phenomenon in China, I would ask for his or her indulgence.

End Notes

1. Google: Catholic Encyclopedia: the Church in China.
2. Sandra Kirby, Experience, *Research, Social Change: Methods from the Margins*. Toronto: Garamond Press, 1989, p.54.

PART ONE

HISTORICAL AND CONTEMPORARY ISSUES OF CHRISTIANITY IN CHINA

CHAPTER I

INTRODUCTION

Contemporary China in Perspective

On the 8th day of the 8th Month (August) in 2008 people around the world watched with disbelief and amazement the spectacular opening of the Olympic Games in Beijing, China. I was lucky to be able to attend this function in the "Bird's Nest" – the newly constructed National Stadium in Beijing and one of the world's most daunting structures. Along with millions of TV viewers around the world, I watched with awe the vast ancient Chinese scrolls being unrolled by high-tech electronics to reveal the high points of Chinese history. I was captivated by the creative dancing of the performers to convey the Chinese idea of Harmony, and dazzled by over 2000 husky artists staging precise martial arts movements. Moments later the flying athletes and the scampering torchbearer galloping in the air mesmerized everyone with disbelief. Indeed, this opening ceremony made us wonder if a new Tang Dynasty has begun in China. The old Tang Dynasty from 618 to 907 represents the peak of Chinese civilization; it was a period of prosperity and great cultural accomplishment unparalleled by any Western achievement of the time.

Equally breath-taking was the closing ceremony. The next morning in the hotel lobby I was able to read comments of the Games in the leading national and international papers Remarks such as the following are worth noting: "…These Olympics showed an open China, a rising China and a peace-loving China;… China has learned about the world and the world has learned about China; … a milestone in China's rising to international status and a historical event in the great renaissance of the Chinese nation…" In fact, the Olympics have brought enormous pride to China and, in the course of it have united all the Chinese both inside and outside the country. Perhaps this Olympics can be perceived as a big step in realizing that China desires to be recognized as a great world power and is eager to become integrated as a part of the world community.

Following the post Olympic glow a few weeks later on September 26 China again surprised the world by its third manned spaceflight mission. As a developing country, it was not a small feat for China to successfully launch its spaceship Shenzhou 7.

China has a span of close to 5000 years of written history consisting of 12 dynasties. Throughout the 19th and the first half of the 20th centuries China suffered great humiliation by the West and Japan. The current Peoples' Republic was established by the Chinese Communist Party on October 1st, 1949 under the leadership of Mao Zedong. Since then China went through almost thirty years of social turmoil and economic uncertainty. Finally China as a sleeping giant woke up by 1980, and as predicted by Napoleon in the early 1800's, it has now impressed the world by its peaceful emergence as a world power from historical humiliations. Its economic reform for the last thirty years is impressive beyond doubt.

Political and Economic Perspective

For the first 30 years of Communist rule from 1949 to 1979 China was a closed nation, and was isolated from the outside world. The average income of people was roughly equivalent to 10 eggs, 3.5 lbs of rice, or 2 lbs of meat per day. Generally speaking this average income was the lowest since the year 1795. (1) After the death of Mao, Deng Xiaoping became the leader and initiated the phase of economic reform (1978-1992). He was often quoted as saying, "It doesn't matter if a cat is black or white, just as long as it catches mice". His pragmatic approach was successful to develop the productive force and to liberate the vital power of the people. During this period the progress was steady and balanced without much bureaucratic corruption. The nation as a whole had a high hope of future political reform as well. In fact the state held its 13th Party Congress and let go many restrictions. On the other hand, it encouraged individual initiatives in private enterprising. But the 1989 Tiananmen Square Incident in Beijing, plus the disintegration of the Soviet Union and the downfall of the Communist government in Poland, put a complete stop to such hope. The second phase of economic reform began in 1992 focusing on privatization to this day. Political reform has remained stagnant and the party leadership has no faith in the Western style of democracy for China. The October 2008 meltdown of the global financial crisis has confirmed the thinking of the leadership that the Chinese model of emphasizing stability and growth, not political reform, is correct. (2)

To achieve modernization Beijing has adopted a new strategy which employs one party politics for governance but capitalism for economical development. To sustain this course of action the government has now required that all policies for the country should consist of this identity known as the "Chinese Characteristics".

As a loose term "Chinese Characteristics" means suitability for the Chinese masses. In the social or political context it may mean that the common good takes priority over the individual rights, and the interest of the state should come before those of the individual. Furthermore, the leadership tends to apply the political philosophy of Confucius, China's great pundit who lived in the fifth century B.C.E. According to Confucius, the covenant between the government and the governed necessitates those in authority to provide for the well-being and security of the people, and in return the people have the obligation to submit to a benevolent and just government. Such political philosophy is very alien to the Western democratic values of the dignity and freedom of the individual. Indeed, according to the Christian concept, everyone is created in the image of God and has inherent basic rights. The story of the crucifixion of Christ clearly asks the question if it is alright to sacrifice an innocent person in order to achieve the good of a bigger group.

To affirm its autocratic stance, it was therefore not surprising that on October 19th, 2005 China issued its first white paper on political democracy. It states that China's "basic principle that the Marxist theory of democracy must be combined with the reality of China...The Communist Party of China's leadership and rule is needed for uniting hundreds of millions of people to work in concerted efforts in building a beautiful future." In short, Beijing reaffirmed the one-party rule, although it has occasionally allowed local political elections at the village or town level.

Economic Growth

Economically China is determined to become a middle-class society and is making effort to provide its 1.3 billion people with a lifestyle more or less equal to that of the West. Such middle class lifestyle is undreamed of by anyone in China, except perhaps by those close relatives of overseas

Chinese in Western Europe and North America. The fact is that, in the course of 30 years, to date 300 million people in China have become the new middle class in the urban centers mostly on the coastal plains. It is not a small feat to realize this dream. The speed and success of China's economic development have caused alarm to some analysts who wondered if the earth has enough resources to continue to sustain the Chinese dream for the other 800 millions.

For example, in 2007 the gross domestic product (GDP) of China was 2.4 trillion US dollars, the 4th largest in the world. In 1998 China was not on the list of top 10 trading nations of the world. In 2008 it has become the world's 3rd largest nation for international trade, and has earned the title "Factory of the World". Its foreign reserve has reached 1.8 trillion US dollars in 2007, and keeps increasing by 100 billion each year. Its per capita income for 2007 has reached US$3,500 for a population of 1.3 billion. The economic progress of China is reflected clearly by the fast development of infrastructure such as highways and airports. Today, 4000 km of express highways are built each year, a length that is sufficient to link the east and west coasts of the United States. However, the gap between the rich and the poor keeps widening. To measure this economic gap the Gini co-efficient index is used by internal agencies. China's Gini co-efficient index is now 0.52, way above the international critical index of 0.37. As an illustration, in 2005 according to the UN report of the level of human development, the western mountain province of Guizhou was the same as the poor West African nation of Namibia, but the central coastal metropolitan city of Shanghai (pop. 18 million) was equal to Portugal. (3) As a result, it is not uncommon that people take to the street to complain about their woes and grievances, particularly the unjust appropriation of lands and houses for urban and industrial developments. For example, in 2007 there were 90,000 such demonstrations over the country, and all levels of the government were very alarmed.

In the short span of thirty years China has completed both its industrial and information revolutions, which the West has taken more than two hundred years to conclude. For further modernization to realize, the Chinese authorities have resorted to autocracy for achieving internal stability and security, to the extent that violations of human rights become inevitable. The leadership is very hung up on internal stability, so much so that in the vast territory of China there is only one time zone to avoid confusion. Furthermore, inherent in the concept of "Chinese Characteristics" is the inclusion of fundamental Chinese culture in its social and religious developments, free from foreign dominations.

Moral Vacuum

However, in this hurry to accomplish national dignity and sovereign security, the Chinese people have experienced unprecedented turmoil of their social values, the worst of which is the development of a moral vacuum whereby greed and self-interest have become the norm of most people at the expense of social conscience. This moral decay is particularly serious considering the vast population of 1.3 billion, because one small problem can become 1.3 million larger. (4) Consequently, a series of problems have taken place such as environmental degradation, a huge rift between the rich and the poor manifested particularly in a big rural-urban divide, devastation of basic human rights, especially the unfair appropriation of private lands and houses by investors to make room for modern buildings, with the backing of corrupt local government officials.

The general feeling of the people in contemporary Chinese society is a mixed one. While most people are proud that China is now emerging as an international power, a great many have developed a deep sense of hopelessness or loss of trust in human relationship. This comes particularly from the evil of greed at every level of society. The situation has become so bad that for every two minutes in China, one person has committed suicide. (5) People would take advantage of each other only if they would make a profit. The most alarming incident was milk powder and formula tainted with the industrial compound of melamine to disguise diluted milk in order to make a bigger profit. This caused several infant deaths, and 53,000 babies became sick with kidney stones as reported by most media in September of 2008. (6) This is particularly alarming to the parents under the current one child policy. The public was outraged when they suspected that Chinese local authorities refused to order a recall of the product after they had known of the poisoned milk ingredients. The national government in China is a very centralized one. Often local governments would not follow orders from above because the bureaucracy is too stupendous and local concerns would not become a priority.

The leadership is aware of the problem but no single leader is capable of revamping this huge governmental machinery as the Communist ideology has become so ingrained among older party members who wanted to keep the status quo and would not want to relinquish the power of the party. On several occasions and as recently as September 25, 2008 when he addressed the United Nations Assembly, Premier Wen Jiabao sadly mentioned, with reference to his terms of office since the year 2000, that the nation is always beset with both natural or man-made disasters and that the nation should learn from problems and become more resilient He was referring to the SARS health issue in 2003, the high rate of HIV/AIDS among the poor, the abnormally cold weather causing crop failure in 2007, the global recall of toys containing lead, the Sichuan earthquakes in 2008, and now the tainted milk products scandal. Other issues for China, according to Wen, are many, including the environment, energy and resource supplies, and rule by law and democracy for China. As the population of China is so large (more than 1.3 billion) he pointed out that one small problem can become 1.3 billion larger for the nation. While this is true of the situation in China, the basic question is: what to do with the abating traditional values in the Chinese society today.

The Role of Christianity in Contemporary Chinese Society

So what is the remedy for the moral vacuum in China today? Although Christianity has been considered a foreign religion by the Chinese, yet more and more people in China today are attracted to the Christian message to fill their interior void. Traditional Chinese philosophy and religious beliefs such as Confucianism, Daoism and Buddhism are more concerned with self-cultivation and spiritual development rather than the transformation of society. Christianity, on the other hand, has been found able to transform the lives of many people. In my encounter with Christians in China many have told me that after becoming committed Christians they have experienced a personal transformation in the present morality void, particularly from inferiority, desperation, depression, and hopelessness into self-confidence, self-esteem, spiritual fulfillment, and a sense of righteousness. Particularly those in the rural areas have told me that they have become self-restraining and unselfish in helping each other. In short, Christianity is replacing their selfish desires with faith, hope and love. It has demonstrated contributions which other religions in China have not been able to make. In short, Christianity has met the needs of an increasing number of the people, especially in their loss of hope concerning their future.

A Popular Religion

A great number of people I interviewed claimed that by believing in Christ they have developed their moral courage and become new persons. In fact, what they said is in agreement with St. Paul's teaching in Ephesians 4: 21-24. When they told me that Christianity brings salvation from sin and a change of heart, they were referring to 1 Timothy 4:9-10. They shared that Christianity would help develop their social conscience and guilt feeling, and that law cannot control everything in life, thus indirectly quoting Philippians 1:20, for the law and regulation only aim to control and punish but do not change the heart. As one worshipper told me after church, he felt he had recovered his soul, regained his inner peace and freedom. Some were so moved during hymn singing at the Sunday service that they broke down into tears. When asked why they were so moved, their response was that they had simply found love in Christ in their hopelessness. The older generation especially felt that they were liberated from the yoke of bitterness and injustice inherited from the previous class struggles during the Cultural Revolution. Now they have developed a spirit of forgiveness by a spiritual rebirth. Hence, they felt they have a mission to rebuild the moral foundation of society by denouncing self-interest and greed.

Today, according to the Director of China's State Administration for Religious Affairs, unofficially there are nearly 130 million Christians in 2008. [7] He further pointed out that "there used to be a saying 'One more Christian is one less Chinese...' Today nobody says that anymore. It is no longer a foreign religion. It is something that belongs to the people. Registered churches are in the hundreds" [8] However, Christianity is not a new religion in China. It was first introduced into China as early as 86 CE according to a recent archeological find [9] Yet how do we account for the fact that over the span of almost 2000 years and in a population of more than 1.3 billion people, the percentage of Christians (Protestant and Catholic) is only 1 per cent. Even Islam has made a more successful inroad into China, with adherents of about 3 per cent, according to the Canadian Global Almanac 2006. The question naturally comes to our mind: Why has Christianity failed to take root in China?

European Christianity

All religions have their own characteristics by geographic location, by the way they are organized, and by their unique theology. As far as Christianity is concerned, the general understanding is that it began after the death of Christ in ancient Palestine near Jerusalem. His disciples, in particular Paul and Peter, spread his teaching around the Mediterranean and after a series of persecutions and other events it began to take root in Rome by the year 313 when the Roman Emperor, Constantine, granted religious freedom to all. In the late 300's it became the state religion of the Roman Empire.

As a Church it began to model its structure and hierarchy after the Roman Empire. It began also to develop its ideology and theology. Apart from the establishment of Eastern Orthodox Churches in 1054, by and large Christianity has developed since the Reformation in 1500's into two main churches: the Roman Catholic and the Protestant. For the convenience of our discussion in this book, we call their evangelism European or Western Christianity.

European Christianity is recognized mainly by their origin, organizational structure and by their ideology and theology. In general they are organized entities, authoritative and would not consider native cultures as equal to their own for the purpose of evangelism. In fact, they rejected the idea of developing indigenous churches with full autonomy in their mission territory. It is in this perspective that we discuss the failure of Christianity to take root in Chinese soil.

Recent development of Christianity in China since 1978 is precluded in our discussion of Christian failure.

Failure of Christianity to Inculturate in China

There are a number of reasons why Christianity has not made sufficient inroads in China, but the most important and subtle one is the inability to inculturate, or to accommodate the Chinese culture, including political harmonization. Until recently from the 16th Century, Christian missionaries in general had considered native cultures including religions as inferior to that of the West. A sense of European racial superiority had prompted the attitude among Western politicians and missionaries to order the world according to their culture. This was particularly the mentality of the Spanish and Portuguese missionaries when they evangelized South America, the Philippines and Africa. All non-Christian cultures were considered as being the work of the devil and perhaps had to be destroyed. (10)

In a similar manner after China was defeated by Britain in the infamous Opium War in 1842, Europe began to colonize China. Christian missions, both Catholic and Protestant alike, became a part of the unequal treaties forced on the people in this land of high culture. Christianizing now meant colonizing, and missionaries made sure that Western civilization and culture dominated the church. It is small wonder that since then, deep in the hearts of many Chinese people, Christianity has had the image of an imperialistic foreign religion, and opposition to it among the general populace has become natural.

I would like to end this brief introduction by quoting the observation of an important official of the Chinese Catholic Patriotic Association, for our reflection on failure of European Christianity to take root in China: (11)

> There is no use hiding the fact that in many ways we are still copying the model of Western Christianity. There are still many things which do not correspond to the customs of China. We have not yet constructed an indigenous system of evangelization or theology that is adapted to conditions of China and the spirit of our generations…that is why we must build a Chinese Catholic Church by going back to the source of the Bible, the apostolic tradition, the Chinese realities which will reflect the true face of our country.

Similarly Aloysius Jin Luxian of Shanghai, a strong and enlightened leader of the Chinese Catholic Church, concurs with Wang Hao and has this to say: (12)

> The reason why the Chinese people in the past did not easily accept Christianity is not only because the Catholic Church was too foreign in its organization and system. It was also because the theological system that is preached was practically a product of the integration of the Gospel with Hellenistic philosophy and Roman culture. Making use of Aristotelian logic to express a theological system of thought with the concepts of rights and duties of the Latin culture as a framework is really rather incongruous with Chinese tradition which has humaneness, justice and morality as the core of its system of thought. It is no wonder that it was not easily acceptable to the Chinese people.

THE DRAGON AND THE CROSS

Chapter I

INTRODUCTION

End Notes

1. Li Yonggang, "Uncertain Prosperity: a Political Scientist's Analysis of Thirty Years of Reform in China", translated by Michael J. Sloboda, in *Tripod*, Autumn 32008, p.19
2. Geoffrey York, "Comments", *Globe and Mail*, 2008 Oct 17, p. A13. See also, Liu Ruishao, A General Discussion of China's 30 years of Openness and Reform," translated by Peter Barry, in *Tripod*, Autumn 2008, p. 16.
3. Li Yonggang, Ibid, pp. 18-28
4. In retrospect we can trace this moral void to the Cultural Revolution in China from 1966-1970, When Mao began to encourage the people to accuse each other for not being loyal to his leadership. In order to gain favor people often falsely accused their neighbors, friends, teachers, or employers. Even children were encouraged to incriminate their parents for not following the Communist principles.
5. *World Journal*, 2008 09 10, A12)
6. "53,000 Babies ill in Milk Scandal", National Post, 2008 Sept. 23, A8.
7. Lorna Dueck, "It's been a brutal Olympics for Chinese Olympics," *Globe and Mail*, August 21, 2008, p.A13)
8. I find the responses interesting when I compare them to the book *Is Christianity Good for the World? A Debate* by Christopher Hitchens and Douglas Wilson. Toronto: Mcclellend and Stewart Ltd., 2008; also online christianity-today.com/ct/.)
9. *World Journal*, 2002-08-11, A10 .
10. Hans Kung and Julia Ching. *Christianity and Chinese Religions*. New York: Doubleday & Collins, 1989.
11. Wang Hao, "Allonger le pas sur la voie d'une Eglise independante et autonome," translated into French by Jean Charbonnier in "La sinisation de l'Eglise chinoise" in Exchange France-Asie, no.1/88, Paris, January 1988, pp. 2-8.

12. "A small boat on the Boundless Ocean – The future of the Catholic Church in Mainland China." A presentation published in the Yi China Message, and reprinted in the Sedos Bulletin (Rome), vol. 27 no. 4, April 15, 1995.

CHAPTER II

A HISTORICAL PERSPECTIVE OF CHINA, WITH PARTICULAR EMPHASIS ON THE 16TH AND 17TH CENTURIES DURING THE EUROPEAN RENAISSANCE

For us to understand the Chinese as a nation we need to know its general historical background and how events developed there.

Written records of Chinese history date from the Shang dynasty (1766?-1122 B.C.). Distinctive Chinese culture developed from the central valley of the Huang Ho (Yellow River) about 3000 B.C., and gradually spread over most of China proper. The Shang kingdom developed around the Huang Ho Valley and became a highly developed society with a government of hereditary aristocrats. Among its contributions to civilization was the establishment of a system of Chinese writing.

The Shang dynasty was overthrown in 1122 B.C. by the Chou people of western China. The new Chou dynasty ruled China until 256 B.C. At the beginning, the Chou government directly controlled part of northern China only. In the east, it gave authority to some followers. Later, these chosen followers formed their own independent states and became disobedient to the royal court. The Chou rulers were further weakened by non-Chinese invaders from the north and the west, and were forced to move their capital from Sian to Loyang.

The eastern independent states fought each other during the later Chou period for the control of all China, particularly between 403 and 221 B.C. Chinese society was being disintegrated by the fighting and disorders. Many people came up with ideas to maintain social order, including magical and religious standards. Confucius the philosopher proposed new moral standards to restore social order. The rulers were convinced by his teachings and accepted his moral code of ethics. This new development of Chinese thought can be compared to the shift from religion to philosophy in the history of Greece at about the same time.

By 221 B.C. the Ch'in or Qin (秦) state was able to unify all other smaller states into one empire with a strong central government. Since then, successive dynasties and rulers were able to govern China up to the end of the Ch'ing or Qing (清) dynasty by using a combination of Confucian moral values, authoritarianism, strict laws and efficient administration to govern China.

During the history of Chinese dynasties up to 1911, there were two major periods when China was ruled by non-Han (or non-Chinese) monarchs. The Mongols gained control of all China in 1279 but was overthrown by Chu (朱) (Han Chinese) in 1368 when the Ming dynasty was established. But Ming China was invaded and defeated by the foreign Manchu from northeast China. The Manchu or the Ch'ing dynasty lasted from 1644 to 1911. This last dynasty was replaced by the Republic of China by a revolution led by Dr. Sun Yat-Sun in 1912. Later Mao Tse-tung led a communist revolution and in October 1949 established the Peoples Republic of China.

Timeline of the Major History of China

As a good understanding of the general dynasties of China is important for the understanding of the discussion, a timeline of the major history of China is therefore given below: (1)

1766? - 1122 B.C.	China's first dynasty, the Shang, rule the nation. (商)
1122 B.C.	The Zhou (Chou) people of western China (周) overthrew the Shang and set up a new dynasty that rule until 256 B.C.
221-206 B.C.	The Qin (Ch'in) dynasty (秦) established China's first strong central government.
206 B.C.-A.D.220	China became a powerful empire under the Han dynasty. (漢) Chinese culture flourished.
581 - 618	The Sui dynasty reunified China after almost 400 years of division. (惰)
618 - 907	The T'ang dynasty ruled China during a period of prosperity and great cultural accomplishment. (唐)
960 - 1279	The Song (Sung) dynasty ruled the empire and made Neo-Confucianism the official state philosophy. (宋)
1275 - 1292	Marco Polo visited China.
1279 - 1368	The Mongols gained control of all China and established the Yuan Dynasty (元)
1368 - 1644	The Ming dynasty governed China. Ricci arrived Macao in 1583. (明)
1644 - 1912	The Manchu ruled China as the Qing (Ch'ing) dynasty. (清)
1911 - 1949	The Republic of China, first under the leadership of Dr. Sun Yat-Sun (孫中山) and later under the leadership of Chiang Kai-Shek (蔣介石)
1949 –	Mao Zedong (毛澤東) established the People's Republic of China under Communist rule

As the discourse in this book deals mainly the Ming and Ch'ing dynasties, a brief description of these two dynasties become necessary.

The Ming Dynasty

The first Ming Emperor Chu overthrew the foreign Mongols in 1368 by organizing insurrections in central China. The Ming Dynasty ruled China from 1368 to 1644, and up to the first part of the 17th Century, enjoyed a period of relative stability and prosperity. Because of their long and continuous cultural tradition, the Chinese had long considered themselves culturally superior, but not on the basis of race or nationalism, and definitely not on militancy. This was in sharp contrast to the European attitude of that time. The European nations believed in their superiority as a chosen race, and set apart with a will to conquer, colonize and to proselytize Christianity.

Throughout the history of China, including that of Ming and Ch'ing periods, occasionally Chinese military power extended over its boundaries. But such expansion was undertaken not for the sake of conquering, but for resisting or expelling the 'barbarians' who threatened the sovereignty of China. The Chinese rulers were content when Chinese cultural superiority and sovereignty were recognized through the tribute missions. As an illustration, during the reign of the Ming emperor Yung-Lo from 1405 on for twenty eight years, he commissioned the Senior Eunuch Zheng He (Ch'ang Ho) (鄭和) to lead a seven great maritime expeditions with fifty or more of big junks and about twenty-seven thousand men to go to the coast of the Malayan Peninsula and as far west as Africa to promote the cultural prestige of Ming China. (2) To this day, Ch'ang has left important landmarks on Malaysia, in particular the port of Malacca.

When Ch'ang Ho expeditions were completed in 1433, China began to isolate herself from further contact with the outside world. This was the first self-imposed cultural isolation in the history of China, because when China was under the cosmopolitan Mongol rule during the Yuan Dynasty (1280-1368), China was part of the huge Mongol Empire, stretching from the Yellow Sea to the Dyneper River in Europe and beyond.

When Ming rulers shook off the Mongol yoke, they felt the need to protect the "organic whole" of the Chinese values by isolating China from any outside influences, and by establishing a monolithic orthodoxy. As Leys points out:

> Chinese universe has always appeared as an organic whole, but it is only since the Ming that the civilization of the organic whole became totalitarian. Under the Han (206 B.C to A.D.220), the T'ang (618 - 906) and the Sung (960 - 1279), China's totalitarian regimes were not despotic; a wide and fruitful margin of expression was allowed to minority or opposition groups ... With the Ming this all changed drastically. The emperor took on absolute power and he exercised it not through ministers and the traditional high administration but through his eunuchs and private servants. A career in politics, which for two thousand years (practically since the time of Confucius!) had been the privilege and responsibility of the scholar elite, became a cesspool from which honest men recoiled in disgust, and fled in fear. At the same time the rigid control over public opinion exercised by the Ming regime condemned intellectual life to dogmatism, paralysis and sterility...As a corollary, and crowning their totalitarian enterprise, the Ming then cut off China from all external contacts. The famous sea expeditions of Cheng Ho were ventures of empty prestige, with no cultural or economic significance, and cannot be compared with the flourishing maritime activities of the Sung Dynasty. (3)

The western image of a static-and-hermetic China was a reflection of the situation created by the Ming and perpetuated by the Ch'ing Dynasty (1644-1912). Such image had never been the image of China under the Han, the T'ang, the Sung, and even the Yuen. "China's power of invention, evolution and adaptation... its creative genius, its political, economic and cultural vitality were both the result and cause of a civilization that was essentially open and frankly cosmopolitan." (4)

Small wonder Ming emperors despised all foreign things. By late Ming, the Japanese pirates (wako) were already troubling the Chinese coasts. When Portuguese, Dutch and Spanish traders visited ports in southern China during the 1500's and 1600's, the Ming officials treated them as inferiors, and under the influence of the wako, considered the trade activities of these Europeans to be more smuggling and piracy. (5) Such low opinions of the European traders made it very difficult for the Jesuits to start their missionary activities in China, for they were considered partners of the European traders. We have to understand clearly that when western historians labelled China as "Xenophobia" and "Sino-centrism" they referred to the particular characteristic of China since the Ming Dynasty but not before.

Soon the successive Ming emperors gave themselves over to pleasure and did not even hold court for dozens of years. Imperial powers and high level administration, as noted before, fell into the hands of the senior eunuchs because they were very close to the emperors' daily lives. As a result, corruption and lawlessness became rampant in China, leading to the downfall of the Ming Dynasty in 1644 when first, the rebels attacked the Forbidden Palace, and soon the Manchu invaded Peking and occupied the important cities. The Ch'ing Dynasty thus replaced the Ming.

The Manchu or Qing (Ch'ing) Dynasty

The Manchu were foreigners from north-eastern China, but unlike the Mongols who never took up any Chinese (Han) culture, the Manchu had adopted many Chinese cultural elements such as language, writing, literature and the classics, even before they gained control of China. As a result, the Manchu rulers continued the administrative philosophy of the Ming Dynasty - supporting neo-Confucianism as the state philosophy and using the Ming administrative model.

From 1661 to 1799 under the first three emperors of K'ang-his (康禧), Yung-cheng (雍正) and Kien-lung (乾隆), the Ch'ing Empire experienced stability and prosperity. Military expeditions were sent out to Mongolia, Tibet, and central Asia. The economy prospered with high agricultural production, and the development of trade and home industries of handicrafts. Population had expanded to about 400 million by 1850.

The Ch'ing Dynasty started to decline from the end of the 18th Century, as agricultural production fell behind population growth. The emperors and royal court members gave themselves over to pleasure, and the country began to be plagued by political corruptions and economic recessions. Anti-Machu secret groups were formed to start rebellions, the most well-known of which was the Taiping Rebellion. There were also clashes with foreign powers, particular with the British over the issue of opium smuggling by British traders of the East Indian Company. As a result, the infamous Opium War took place between China and Britain. China was defeated and forced to sign the Treaty of Nanking whereby Hong Kong was ceded to Britain in 1842. More unequal treaties were forced on China by the foreign powers, including the United States, Russia and Japan. But it is beyond the scope of this thesis to go into historical details. We are mainly concerned with that part of Chinese history that shows the background against which the first Jesuit mission came in 1583 and was expelled in 1742.

Buddhism, Confucianism and the Chinese Society

Both Ming and Ch'ing dynasties used the Confucian code of ethics as the guiding principle to rule and maintain the Chinese society. High level civil servants were selected by their passing a strict examination on the Confucian Classics. By taking such civil examinations, the candidates were expected to show their knowledge of the Classics to solve administrative problems. In order to climb the social ladder, parents would send their children to Confucian tutors to study the Classics. The Chinese social hierarchy consisted of five stratifications starting with the scholars at the top, thereafter came the farmers, the manufacturers, the merchants and finally the soldiers at the bottom. As everyone aspired to become scholars, it was small wonder that for both dynasties, an elite class of literati was formed. They were looked up to by everyone. Whatever they believed or did, they would certainly be copied by others on the social scales.

But the Confucian code of ethics over the centuries was unable to fill a religious vacuum in China. Daoism (Taoism 道教) is a native Chinese religion but it talks more of withdrawal from daily life and living in harmony with nature than about human sufferings and the meaning of life. Taoism throughout the ages has come to include elements of folk beliefs, so it has become a religion with many protective gods and spirits. It became a religion in China at about the same time as Confucius was delivering his philosophical and ethical messages over the different warring states by the end of the Chou Dynasty. As people could not find solutions to the many problems of life in Taoism, Buddhism was welcomed into China from India during the peak of T'ang, about 500 years after the birth of Christ. When Buddhism talked about compassion, reincarnation, the cause-effect meaning of suffering, the emptying of one's life to pursue peace of mind and the highest state of life, it became a very enlightening religion to the Chinese. However, long before Buddhism was introduced into China, the Chinese were already practising folk religion and Taoism. Once in China, Buddhism began to change its original form and theology by accommodating all other religions in China. Thus in Chinese Buddhism, we find a mix of Taoism and Shamanism as well.

To understand why the Chinese were able to accept a new religion so well such as Buddhism, we must turn to the geography and the early civilization of China for an answer. This is important and helps us to understand why Christianity failed in China after all the hard work of Ricci and the Jesuit Mission.

First let us look at the geography of China. The Chinese civilization developed in north central China along the Yellow River (Huang-Ho), known as the cradle of Chinese civilization. At the lower course of the Huang-Ho is the great North China Plain where over the centuries before the birth of Christ, the civilization had become mature, and recorded history had come into being. To the north of this plain are the Mongolian uplands with the Gobi Desert not far away. To the west are the Tibetan Highlands with the many mountain ranges running down to the south and southeast. To the south are the central uplands with the Yangtze River beyond, and further away are the Pearl River and the South China Sea. To the east is that part of the Pacific Ocean known as the China Sea. As an agricultural society, one can understand that the earlier Chinese could find no better place to expand their territory perhaps somewhat only to the south where more plains were formed by the Yangtze and the Pearl River. As agricultural people, they did not want to expand to the northern frontier where the Mongolian landscapes dominate, nor would they want to expand to the west where the Tibetan terrains were hostile to farming. So they were satisfied to stay in the north China plain that they developed a unique nature of 'accommodation'. In other words, to make life easier physically or spiritually, the early Chinese did not develop an aggressive attitude for their survival such as conquering or exploring other lands. Instead, they decided to utilize and internalize whatever they already had to improve their lives, thus forming an "inward looking" life style. For example, during the warring states period in their early history, the warlords would prefer to find peace by intermarriage among their families. By marrying the daughter of the neighbouring warlord, the two states became relatives, and thus peace, or at least truce, was achieved. (6)

Thus the concept of 'harmony' became more important than that of subjugation or conquest. There was no corresponding Chinese counterpart of the typical European attitude of conquest and subjugation of that time. The Chinese never wanted any direct impact of any foreign ideas. They would only accept new cultural elements in a less direct and subtle way such as the development of relationships. No doubt, cultural pride had so much to play here, and this explains why they called themselves the Middle Kingdom, meaning the centre of the world's civilizations.

By the same token when Buddhism was introduced into China, the Chinese were already practising Taoism and Shamanism; and instead of saying one religion was right and the other was wrong, they were able to harmonize all beliefs into one. Buddhism, on the other hand, was willing to accommodate other religious elements according to the thinking of the Chinese. Thus it was welcome and accepted by the Chinese, none the less it had to take on a new form and perhaps a new belief system. Indeed in China, historical figures of loyalty to the countries such as Kuan-kung (關公 God of War) were even syncretised into the belief system as a Bodhisattva.

CHAPTER II

A HISTORICAL PERSPECTIVE OF CHINA IN THE 16TH AND 17TH CENTURIES DURING THE EUROPEAN RENAISSANCE

End Notes

1. For general information on the history of China, consult *Encyclopaedia Britannica*.
2. Joseph Sebes, S.J. *A "Bridge" Between East and West: Father Matteo Ricci, S.J. His Times, His Life, and His Methods of Cultural Accommodation*. Rome: Historical Institute of the Society of Jesus, [1978], p.6. See also: *Proceedings of the International Symposium on Chinese-Western Cultural Interchange in commemoration of the 400th Anniversary of the Arrival of Matteo Ricci, S.J. in China*. Taipei, Taiwan: University of Fujen Press, 1984 (preface).
3. Simon Leys. *China Shadows*. New York: Doubleday, 1977, pp 208-210. Cited in Joseph Sebes, S.J. *Ibid.*, pp 6-7.
4. *Ibid*.
5. Bernard Hung-key Luke, "The Background in European History of Matteo Ricci's Mission", *Tripod*, Vol. 12, 1982, pp82-84.
6. Y.S.Leung. *Christianity and Chinese Religions* (Audio Tape), Edmonton: Chinese [Christians] Outreach, 1990.

CHAPTER III

CONFUCIUS' MORAL TEACHING AND ITS RELATIONSHIP TO CHRISTIANITY

In our previous chapters, we have discussed that for over two thousand years one teaching permeated and dominated the political and social life of China. It was the teaching of Confucius. Therefore successful Christian evangelization must accommodate the moral teaching of Confucius as there are many similarities between the Christian moral teaching and that of Confucius. At the world Synod of Bishops on the Bible Oct. 15, 2008 Cardinal Zen of Hong Kong said that "...the Church in China must engage in dialogue and work with those who defend the traditional values found in Confucianism...The traditional Chinese wisdom founded in and fostered by Confucianism contains the 'seed of the word' of God that the Second Vatican Council said are present in religions and cultures...If, moved by charity, we are able to instil in the younger generation the Chinese virtues of fidelity, honesty and shame, we will have helped them take a big step toward holiness. " (1)

Biographical Background
Exactly who was Confucius and what was his teaching about? Confucius is the Latinized form of his commonly

known name K'ung Fu-Tsu, or Master K'ung. His real name was K'ung Chung-ni. He was born near Ch'u-fu in today's Shangtung in China. In Chapter I we have discussed briefly the early history of China. The Chou Dynasty from 1122 B.C. underwent years of chaos and disorder due to internal unrests and external invasions. Society was disintegrating, and people everywhere suffered. Such conditions could be compared to the state of the Israelis in the Hebrew Bible waiting for a Messiah to deliver them out of misery. Many people came up with ideas to restore social order, including magical and religious standards. Among them was Confucius who proposed new moral standards to restore political and social order. He travelled extensively over ten years to visit many feudal states of his time, hoping to find a ruler who would use his advice, but his hope was never realized. At his death he was relatively unknown in China, and it was his disciples who recorded his ideas (in conversations and sayings) in a book commonly known as The Analects.

Confucius was born near Ch'u-fu in today's Shangtung in China. Like Jesus Christ, little was known about his early life. The highest public office ever held by him was police commissioner for about a year in his small home state of Lu when he was fifty. He travelled extensively beyond his own state in his old age to preach his ideas of social order, hoping to find a ruler who would use him to implement his ideas. As he was not able to achieve his goal, he devoted instead his time to teach his disciples, while furthering his interest in music and poetry.

We can understand Confucius' personality and mission by reading the following verses from the Analects 2:4, which was a record of his conversations with his disciples. (2)

> At fifteen I set my heart on learning [to be a sage].
> At thirty I became firm.
> At forty I had no more doubts.

At fifty I understood Heaven's Will.
At sixty my years were attuned [to this Will].
At seventy I could follow my heart's desires without overstepping the line.

Confucius was well known for his regard for rituals in the Book of Li-Ching from which we understand his appreciation of the virtue of propriety. We can also discern his profound sense of religion as indicated by his reverence for the will of Heaven in the above quote.

But Confucius lived in an age of social turmoil, and as in our contemporary life, people in his time questioned the ancient religious beliefs. Humanist philosophers would stay away from the emphasis on divination and sacrifice, and it was Confucius who was able to introduce philosophical reflections in an atmosphere of rationalism.

In addition to the Analects or Lun-yu (論語), the Five Classics are considered as the basic texts of Confucianism. They include the Book of Changes or Yi-jing (I-Ching 易經), the Book of History or Shu-jing (Shu-ching, 書經), the Book of Poetry or Shi-jing (Shik-ching 詩經), the Classic of Rites (禮記 Li-ching), and the spring and Autumn Annals or Chun-qiu (Ch'un -ch'iu 春秋). The Book of Music, often held as the sixth classic, was lost in the course of history. These classics became the basis of state civil examinations during the Han dynasty (202 B.C. to A.D. 220), and Confucianism had thus become state philosophy of China, and hence the tradition, for almost two thousand years until the May 4th Movement in the early part of the Republic after the 1911 revolution. During the May 4th Movement in China, people began to question if Confucianism was a roadblock for China to become modernized as Confucianism had set rigid social roles for the individual, and as an ideology it could enslave rather than liberating the minds for the truth; as such it could thus discourage social change to take place.

However, there is a renewed interest of Confucianism in China, Taiwan, Singapore and South Korea, as witnessed by the strong sense of work ethics in these NICs (Newly industrialised countries), and the new social values being promoted by governments.

It is not possible for us to discuss Confucius' teaching in detail in this chapter, as space does not allow us to do so. However, in order to understand Ricci's work in China, a short discussion of Confucius moral teaching is necessary.

Confucius Moral Teaching

Confucius' teaching of 'Jen' can be arbitrarily translated as humanity (or goodness, benevolence, human-heartedness), and refers more to the inner orientation of the person. It is always concerned with relationships. The 'negative' Golden Rule (Analects 15:23) sums up his entire teaching: "not to do to others what you would not have them do to you" (已所v欲勿施於人). Thus the great merit of Confucianism lies in the moral character of human relationships commonly known as the Confucian Five Cardinal Relations (wu-lun 五倫): (a) ruler-minister (b) father-son (c) husband-wife (d) elder and younger brother, and (e) friend and friend. (3) It becomes clear at once that three are family relationships and even the first and last are based on the family model. Thus the ruler-minister relationship can be perceived in the same manner as father-son, and the friendship in the same way as brotherliness. Therefore in Confucius' teaching, society should consider itself as a large family, as Analects 12:5 points out so well, "Within the four seas all men are brothers" (四海之內皆兄弟也).

We must not overlook the fact that in Confucianism, the responsibilities arising from these relationships are mutual and reciprocal:

A minister owes loyalty to this ruler, and a child filial respect to the parent. But the ruler must also care for his subjects, and the parent for the child. All the same, the Five Relationships emphasize the vertical sense of hierarchy. Even within the horizontal relationship between friends, seniority of age demands a certain respect; and if the conjugal relationship bears more natural resemblance to that between older and younger brothers, it is more usually compared to the ruler-minister relationship. And the duty of filial piety - the need of procuring progeny for the sake of assuring the continuance of the ancestral cult - has been for centuries the ethical justification for polygamy.(4)

One can see at once that in the traditional Chinese society, it is the family rather than the individual that is the centre of life. By letting oneself down unethically by accident or by default, one is bringing shame and dishonour to the family. Furthermore, one's life cannot be considered successful if one's family is in disarray, particularly the offspring. Hence, the success of one's children in society through education has the most consideration in one's life.

It has become clear that Confucius' Jen must be understood in the context of relationships. Jen has a number of characteristics, including loyalty (Zhong/Chung 忠) which is loyalty to one's own heart and conscience; and reciprocity (shu 恕) which is respect of and consideration for others. Superimposed on these two characters is propriety or ritual (li 禮) in relation to social behaviour of all occasions of life, such as wedding, birthday celebrations and funerals.

Thus a man of Jen (the moral gentleman) with all these virtues can be distinguished in his behaviour from the inferior or uncultured members of society. He can project his personal cultivation (修身) to influence others, thus bringing peace and harmony (治平) to society. In the personal context,

Jen indeed can be interpreted as love or affection (ren 仁). However, by transforming it into a universal virtue in a broad sense, the man with Jen can become the sage, or the perfect human being.

Mencius was a great Confucian who lived 321 to 289 B.C. He interpreted Confucius' Jen to include universal love. In the book Mencius 4B:28, he said, "The man of Jen loves others."(仁者人也) In the same book Chapter 7A:46, he continued to say that the man of Jen loves all and everyone. In Chapter 7B:1 he further stated that such a Junzi (Chun-Tzu 君子) or Man or Jen "extends his love from those he loves to those he does not love". To illustrate the concept of the meaning of universal love, a similar story to the parable of the Good Samaritan was also given by Mencius. In the Book of Mencius 2A:6, he gave the example of man seeing a child falling into a well. The natural impulse of compassion in the man was to rescue the child, without thinking of any consequences of praise or blame. (今人乍見孺子將入於井, 皆有惻忍之心). Confucian scholars agree with Mencius that Jen is innate in human nature, but it needs to be cultivated by education and training.

Neo- Confucian philosopher Chu-Hsi (1130-1200 A.D.) in the Song dynasty summarized Confucian Jen succinctly as culmination of all virtues. He states forcefully that all virtues are based on the san-kang wu-lun (five cardinal relationships) which in turn is based on Jen. (百善萬行總於五常, 五常又總於仁) (5)

Next to the teaching of Jen, Confucius also taught ritual. The Chinese word for 'ritual' (li 禮) has a strong religious overtone of worship. The ancestral cult or rite, along with the offer to Heaven the supreme Lord, was very rich in ritual. But it also includes social practices and propriety; by itself it is also regarded as training for virtues and the avoidance of evil. So much was the emphasis put on the ritual that Confucianism has been also known as a "ritual religion" (禮教) (6).

In the teaching of "Li", Confucius stressed the need of having the reverence or the right disposition, so that the ritual would not be performed perfunctorily to the extent that it would become hypocrisy. (Analects 15:17). According to Confucius, a sacrifice is to be performed with the spirits in mind (Analects 3:12). The external observance of the offering of the gifts accompanied by musical performances is only secondary in any ritual practice: "What can rites do for a person lacking in the virtue of humanity (jen)? What can music do for a person lacking in humanity? (Analects 3:3)

In his discourse on the importance of rites, Confucius warned his disciples not to be superstitious. In the performance of rituals, Confucius condemned the use of Yung (佣) or wooden human effigies to serve their masters in the nether world. (7) In Mencius 1A:4, Confucius said that "those who made such figures did not deserve to have posterity". It was a strong condemnation of human sacrifice and superstition, "even when performed symbolically". It was largely based on Confucius' concept of the Lord on High or the Lord of Heaven, and Confucius' teaching of the rites that Ricci argued so strongly that the Chinese ancestral rite was not religious but rather cultural in essence.

Confucianism and Christianity

Indeed, Confucian teaching has so much in common with Christianity that it held Ricci in awe after he had studied it, and he was convinced that the earlier Chinese had a strong belief in the true God, but through the ages the true God was forgotten among various cultural intrusions into China. It was his mission on earth to bring God back to the people of China by bridging these two great teachings together - Confucianism and Christianity - so that not only China, but the world at large would become a better one. The only thing lacking in Confucianism, in the mind of Ricci, is a spiritual dimension of God's selfless love for everyone, for Confucian love is a means to an end which is a perfect social order, whereas God's love has no end by itself. In Ricci's opinion, Christianity could make Confucianism more perfect, and this is what he meant by Pu-yu (補儒), or to "supplement Confucianism".

Confucianism as Ming State Philosophy

Before we end this chapter, we must go back to the late Ming Dynasty to investigate further their political thought. The philosophical thinking of that time had made the Chinese culture impervious to all outside influences, including the Christian message which Matteo Ricci and his Jesuit mission tried so hard to bring to the people of China at this period of history.

Once the Ming Dynasty adopted Confucianism as the state philosophy, to become cultured and accepted in society everyone formally or informally studied Confucius' teaching. However, Confucianism in Ming Dynasty was a different kind of Confucius' teaching. It is known as Neo-Confucianism.

Throughout the ages for almost three thousand years until then, new commentaries had been written on the original Four Books and five Classics, particularly those of Zhu Xi (Chu His 朱喜) in the Song Dynasty. This new school of thought formed what was known as Neo-Confucianism, combining the moral standards of traditional Confucianism with elements of Buddhism and Taoism. However, at the beginning of the Ming Dynasty, Wang Shouren (王守仁) became an important thinker and had written new commentaries. He left the Zhu Xi school of thought and started to promote his own - the Study of the Mind. Such thinking further involved the concepts of Li and Chi. In short, Neo-Confucianism taught that man was a part of the universe out of evolution of the Ch'i, and as such man and the universe ultimately became one entity. There was no such thing as creation or creator. Everything evolved to produce new elements or lives. Man was the master of his own fate - to become good by his own will, and not by any external assistance such as the grace of God. But by being virtuous, man became part of the "Supreme Ultimate giving birth to yin-yang which in turn produced the four elements (8). They in turn gave rise to the eight trigrams (pa-kua) which in turn transformed into all things. Such was the way Neo-Confucianism extended the concepts of evolution as contained in the Book of Changes. Undoubted this teaching had the elements of Buddhism and Taoism.

Such was the prevailing philosophical thinking, and had become very ingrained in the minds of the Ming literati. Indeed such was the formidable barrier between Ricci and the literati. Ricci had to overcome this mindset by developing new theories and explanations to point out that such idea of Li and Ch'i had deviated from the original Confucius' teaching of some three thousand years ago. Although a foreigner in China, he had to study the Chinese Classics very thoroughly in order to show that there was mention of God and creation by Confucius himself, but throughout the ages, due to heterodoxy, men had lost God in their thinking.

CHAPTER III

CONFUCIUS MORAL TEACHING AND ITS RELATIONSHIP TO CHRISTIANITY

End Notes

1. "Church must help preserve Chinese wisdom", Western Catholic Reporter, 2008 Oct 20, p. 1.
2. Hans Kung and Julia Ching. *Christianity and Chinese Religions*. Toronto: Doubleday, 1988, p.67..
3. *Ibid.*, p. 68.
4. *Ibid.*, p. 69.
5. "A Glimpse at Confucianism", *Central Alberta News*, May 5, 1994, p.6
6. Hans Kung, *op. cit.*, p. 70.
7. *Ibid.*, p. 71.
8. Hsu, Ch'ang-chih. *P'o-Hsieh chi [an Anthology of Writings Exposing Heterodoxy]*, 8 chuan, cited in John D. Young, *Christianity and Confucianism*, p.57.

CHAPTER IV

A HISTORICAL PERSPECTIVE OF CHRISTIANITY IN CHINA

After recognizing the basic historical and cultural facts of China in previous chapters, we now turn to the history of Christianity in this ancient land. (1) David Suzuki, a well-known environmental scientist, once said that a good knowledge of the past gives a good understanding of the present (2). With this in mind, this Chapter will lead us to a better knowledge of the church situation in China today.

The history of the Christianity in China has six phases of development (3). The first phase marking the earliest contact of Christianity with the Chinese culture began in 635 C.E. when Nestorian monks arrived in Xian, western capital of China. Recent research by Professor Wang Weifeng of the Union Theological College in Nanjing, China has overthrown this commonly held notion of the year 635 A.D. and has concluded that Christianity actually entered China in the year 86 A.D. He arrived at his verdict by a careful study of the inscriptions and pictures that were carved on a huge stone tablet unearthed at Xian in 1625. This large stone tablet was inscribed with Nestorian icons and verses of the scriptures. Today, we find Nestorian writings on the Messiah in the collection of poems by Yang Lian, unearthed in the caves of

Dunhuang in western China in 1625 (4). Nestorianism stayed in China for a brief period and disappeared when it came under persecution.

The second phase began in 1294 during the Yuen Dynasty, when Franciscan Bishop John of Montecorvino arrived in Beijing during the reign of Kublai Khan, grandson of Genghis Khan who established the Mongol Empire that included China, Korea, Mongolia, Persia (now Iran), Turkestan, and Armenia in the 1100s. Marco Polo also came to China at about this time. No one succeeded Montecorvino after his death. (5)

The third phase of Christian history in China began when Matteo Ricci, a Jesuit Catholic priest, arrived in China in 1583. His policy of theological accommodation won him the respect of the Chinese people. Unfortunately, the Rites Controversy with Rome took away all his effort, and the church came under Chinese persecution in 1705. Since then for almost two hundred years, Christianity was totally wiped out of China until 1842, when Britain, in the infamous Opium War, defeated China. (6)

This began the fourth phase of history of Christianity in China when Christianity became part of imperialism and colonialism. The Communist takeover of China in 1949 began the fifth phase of history of Christianity in China, when the new government persecuted the Church because it was under the domination of outside influences, such as foreign mission societies and the Vatican. The persecution became very severe during the Cultural Revolution when atheism reigned supreme. All religions were considered superstitious and counter-productive to the policy and direction of a liberated New China. It was not only Christianity, but all religions were banned from both private and public life. The Red Guards would enter into homes to search for religious objects including statues, the Christian Cross or the Bible. These were considered illegal and the owners of those objects were taken out of the house and prosecuted on the streets immediately. All temples and churches were closed down to become factories or military storage facilities, and all religious objects in the worshipping places were burned or destroyed.

The death of Mao Zedong in 1976 paved the way for a new era for Christianity in China. Under the leadership of Deng Xiaoping who adopted the Open Door Policy, people were again allowed to worship in the open. This is the sixth and the current phase. Christianity germinated from the ashes and has started to bloom. On the one hand the Protestant Church has embarked on establishing an indigenous Chinese Patriotic Christian Church. On the other hand, the Catholic Church in China is trying very hard to follow the government guideline of establishing an independent church from Rome with elected bishops. Rome has considered this as schism, resulting in constant bickering between Beijing and the Vatican over the authority of the appointment of bishops. As a result, the Official Chinese Catholic Church is beset with a number of canonical issues for staying inside the Universal Catholic Church, and is not doing as well as the Protestant counterpart. Unless agreement is reached between Beijing and the Vatican over the canonical status of the Official Catholic Church in China, the future of the Catholic Church in China is not bright. It will become marginalized and will not grow with new dynamic membership as the Protestant Church.

Both the Official Protestant and Catholic Church are confronted with the challenge of their respective underground (or house) churches. These unofficial and illegal clandestine church communities refuse to accept the jurisdiction of the Official Church, leading to internal schism.

In the following chapters we will discuss how European Christianity failed to take root in China during each phase of the history of Christianity.

Chapter IV

A HISTORICAL PERSPECTIVE OF CHRISTIANITY IN CHINA

End Notes

1. Together with my personal observations and inquiries in China, the following authors have provided information for this chapter. Hans Kung and Julia Ching (1988), *Christianity and Chinese Religions;* Patricia Leung (1992), *Sino-Vatican Relations*.
2. David Suzuki. *The Nature of Things: Galileo and the Age of Reasoning*. Edmonton: Access Educational TV, 1985 (Videotape).
3. These five phases are my own creations according to research design theory in historiography. The periods are identified according to the degree of historical influence by the phenomenon on the people or society in which it took place.
4. See *Truth Monthly*, March 2000, p. 14. (Chinese evangelical publication in Vancouver, Canada.)
5. *Ibid*.
6. The Jesuits were well known for their cultural accommodation methods, contrary to the Portuguese and Spanish who insisted that Christianity in missionary lands should not be adulterated by native culture. Cf. Ho (1996), *Theological and Cultural Accommodation: Matteo Ricci and the Jesuit Mission in China*.

CHAPTER V

INCULTURATION

In our previous discussion of why Christianity failed to take root in China we mentioned several times that Christianity was not able to inculturate in the Chinese soil. What is inculturation after all?

Inculturation is a new term in missiology, and is not the same as enculturation in sociology but very much attuned to it. Formerly, the term Cultural Accommodation was usually used. It became popular after the encyclical Redemptoris Missio of John Paul II in 1990. Simply put, inculturation is the proclamation of the Gospel in ways appropriate to the people in the cultural and social context to accommodate the values, attitudes, beliefs and to harmonize the prevailing political heritage. (1) In our present discussion focuses on this question: What is meant by cultural accommodation in missionary history? To answer that question, let's first ask ourselves what culture is.

When we summarize the meanings of culture from different dictionaries and encyclopaedias, we will have the following key concepts: value systems, a way of living, a way of thinking, religion or belief system, relationships, customs, language expressions, acceptable behaviour patterns, festivals and holidays, music, food, arts and crafts, social structure including political system, and many others. When western missionaries preached the Gospel to the people in a different society from the time of geographic discovery in the 16th Century to the end of the Second World War, they tended to ignore altogether the culture of the people because the missionaries considered their own culture better and superior, particularly in the case of the early Spanish and Portuguese missionaries in their newly discovered lands. Their thinking was "spices and souls" and the Christian faith was the property of the Europeans only. In fact, all non-Christian cultures were considered as being the work of the devil and perhaps had to be destroyed. (2) Small wonder that such a mentality gave them a sense that they were superior, "a chosen race, a royal priesthood, a holy nation, a people set apart." (3) It was not uncommon that converts at the time of their baptisms were given not only a Christian name, but were encouraged to take Portuguese or Spanish surnames, wear Portuguese or Spanish clothes and follow their customs. But this practice was totally contrary to the spirit of the Scripture as we read in the Acts of the Apostles: (4)

> Some men came down to Antioch from Judea and began to teach the brothers: "unless you are circumcised according to Mosaic Practice, you cannot be saved". This created dissension and much controversy between them and Paul and Barnabas. Finally it was decided that Paul, Barnabas and some others should go up to see the apostles and elders in Jerusalem....After much discussion, Peter took the floor and said to the apostles and the elders: "Brothers you know well enough that from the early days God selected me from your number to be the one from whose lips the Gentiles would hear the message of the gospel and believe. God, who reads the hearts of men, showed his approval by granting the Holy Spirit to them just as he did to us. He made no distinction between them and us, but purified their hearts by means of faith also.

Why, then, do you put God to the test by trying to place on the shoulders of these converts a yoke which neither we nor our fathers were able to bear? Our belief is rather that we are saved by the favour of the Lord Jesus and so are they". At that the whole assembly fell silent....It was resolved ....that representatives be ...sent to Antioch along with Paul and Barnabas....They were to deliver this letter:....."It is the decision of the Holy Spirit and ours too, not to lay on you any burden beyond that which is strictly necessary, namely, abstain from meat sacrificed to idols.... and from illicit sexual union. You will be well advised to avoid these things. Farewell.".... When it was read there was great delight at the encouragement it gave.

In keeping with this spirit, some missionaries would determine what Western elements are to be introduced to the people they want to evangelize and what native elements are to be retained as judged by what they saw and experienced in the native community. The objective of so doing is to achieve harmony and peaceful acceptance in the impact-response relationship. This is cultural accommodation, and the best example would be the Jesuits missionaries in Asia in the 16th century.

St. Francis Xavier

When we talk about policy of cultural accommodation by western missionaries in Asia, we will inevitably think of St. Francis Xavier (1506-1552) as a historical case [5], for he was the pioneer of all missionaries to Asia. His approach was to propagate the Christian faith in terms of native customs and rites. In short, the Jesuit method was an 'organic' policy to meet the Asian culture on its own terms, involving the missionary to become an integral part of Japan and China. [6]

By his Japanese experience including the challenge by Buddhist monks, Xavier had learned about the importance of understanding and adopting the local culture for missionary work in China and Japan. For him to be accepted by the various Japanese local authorities (daimyo) he had to adopt the aristocratic appearance. By extension, missionaries should put on the most appropriate garb in terms of respect and acceptance. His debates with Buddhist monks convinced him that future missionaries had to be people of learning, particularly in science. The social structure of Japan and China based on authorities as reinforced by Confucianism necessitated the "top-down" missionary approach. Thus if the emperor was converted, the entire people would follow.

In short, Xavier had developed the 'organic' principle of cultural accommodation (7). Christian missionaries in China and Japan had to reach the people on their own terms and at their own levels; they had to become an integral part of the civilization. One mistake he made in his generalization of the situation in China was the social status of the Buddhist monks. He did not realize that Buddhist monks were not equally respected in Confucius China as in Japan. Thus later Jesuit missionaries following his policy in China had to change to the Confucius scholar's garb for winning respect.

Xavier's immediate successor Alessandro Valignano, in carrying out his instructions, went so far as to order his fellow Jesuits to behave like the natives of the country, meaning that they have to "become Chinese to win China for Christ". (8) However, missionaries had to become aware about how far the cultural compromise could go without changing the essential elements of Christian doctrines.

Thus, in the attempt to inculturate, both the Gospel and the Chinese culture accommodate each other and they are mutually enriched in a syncretistic process. As an example, Confucianism and Christianity should be able to accommodate each other in China. This idea was promoted by Matteo Ricci, the first Jesuit missionary who was able to make all his way to Beijing in January, 1601when other foreigners were prohibited from doing so. He realized that for a successful Christian evangelism, the moral teaching of Confucius must be accommodated as there are many similarities between the Christian moral teaching and that of Confucius. We mentioned earlier that at the world Synod of Bishops on the Bible Oct. 15, 2008 Cardinal Zen of Hong Kong said that "...the Church in China must engage in dialogue and work with those who defend the traditional values found in Confucianism... the traditional Chinese wisdom founded in and fostered by Confucianism contains the 'seed of the word' of God that the Second Vatican Council said are present in religions and cultures...If, moved by charity, we are able to instill in the younger generation the Chinese virtues of fidelity, honesty and shame, we will have helped them take a big step toward holiness. " (9)

In reality, inculturation is not a one-way process. It is a double process as we will see better in our later study of Matteo Ricci in the 17th Century China. On the one hand the Gospel challenged the Chinese culture and required that some values and forms be transformed or purified according to the Gospel yet without losing its cultural identity. On the other hand, the Chinese culture offered positive insights that enrich and modify the way the gospel was expressed, understood and lived. Unfortunately, however, this syncretistic approach was rejected by Rome over the Chinese Rites issue soon after the death of Matteo Ricci.

It is also unfortunate that when a number of Protestant missionaries came to China from in the 19th and 20th Century to preach the Christian message, they too adopted a rigid theological position, even to this day, to consider the Chinese Rites of ancestral veneration (not worship) as heretical. In the minds of a great many Chinese, to become Christian was to cease to remain Chinese. However, a small number of Protestant missionaries in the late 19th Century did made some effort to accommodate the Chinese culture, particularly in their effort to acquire an understanding of the Chinese language and philosophy. The most outstanding in this group was Robert Morrison. When he stepped on Chinese soil in 1807 in Macao and later went to Canton (today's Guangzhou in the southern Province of Guangdong), the first thing he did was to learn the language and to translate the basic Christian tenets into Chinese. (10)

Christianity as an Institutionalized Religion in China

For spreading the Christian message we require an institution or organization called the Church. The two main churches in China are the Catholic and the Protestant. We have to examine if the current church model is suitable for China. A number of theologians have pointed out that when missionaries first introduced Christianity to China, they brought along with them the ecclesial model from the European context of the 16th Century to be used in China. In this model the Church is seen as a perfect society that is not part, nor member, of any other society and is not mingled in any way with any other society. It is so perfect that it is distinct from all human society and stands above it. Consequently it is accountable to no secular authority or jurisdiction. The conflict with a closed culture and an authoritarian government, as in the case of China, is almost unavoidable (11).

The Christian Church, Cultural Accommodation and Political Harmonization

For the Church to become a viable institution in the future, it must be able to accommodate its language, liturgy and theology in the Chinese culture. It must not be perceived as a foreign religion in China. It must develop its Chinese identity, not just in ritual worship, but most importantly in the manner in which they live the Gospel in their daily life. In his effort to Christianize the Chinese people in the 17th Century, Matteo Ricci came under the influence of the

Chinese culture and became "Confucianized" himself. He discovered that the teachings of Confucius were parallel to the teachings of Christ, however with one missing aspect, namely the universal and unconditional love in Christianity. He therefore attempted to supplement Confucianism with Christianity to complete the moral teaching in China. His effort was successful in winning the admiration and support of the literati and the upper class of Chinese society. He was able to give Christianity a Chinese identity for it to take root in Chinese soil.

Today, as China has awakened to stand on its own feet with dignity and pride, the Church has never before now felt so greatly the need to harmonize itself with the Chinese culture. The Chinese people must see undeniably that the Church is truly a Chinese community, and that the Church can project itself with uniqueness beyond its territorial confines to enrich the universal Church.

As the relationship between the Church and culture is so important in this study, I would like to quote again the observations of two contemporary church leaders for our reflection on this matter. Wang Hao is an important official of the Chinese Catholic Patriotic Association and has this to say (12):

> There is no use hiding the fact that in many ways we are still copying the model of Western Christianity. There are still many things which do not correspond to the customs of China. We have not yet constructed an indigenous system of evangelization or theology that is adapted to conditions of China and the spirit of our generation. What Christian message do we announce? How do we spread it? We do not have a solution yet...That is why we must build a Chinese Catholic Church by going back to the sources of the

Bible, the apostolic tradition, the Chinese realities which will reflect the true face of our country.

In the same vein, Bishop Aloysius Jin Luxian of Shanghai, a strong and enlightened leader of the CCC, concurs with Wang Hao (13):

> The reason why the Chinese people in the past did not easily accept Christianity is not only because the Catholic Church was too foreign in its organization and system. It was also because the theological system that it preached was practically a product of the integration of the Gospel with Hellenistic philosophy and Roman culture. Making use of Aristotelian logic to express a theological system of thought with the concepts of rights and duties of the Latin culture as a framework is really rather incongruous with Chinese tradition which has humaneness, justice and morality as the core of its system of thought. It is no wonder that it was not easily acceptable to the Chinese people.
>
> What we must now do is to shed the features of its Greek philosophy and Roman culture and retain the essence of the Gospel and use this to preach to the contemporary people of China. In other words, we are to preach Jesus, His person, His deeds and teaching directly. The words and parables spoken by Jesus are not stark dogmatic doctrine but teachings full of vitality that pull at the chords of the human heart. The Gospel transcends time and space and can be accepted by any person...
>
> Last but not least, political harmonization is now a part of the Chinese culture and is important for the future

survival of the Church. Political harmonization and accommodation with China are perceived as important by other Christian denominations such as the Anglican Church in Hong Kong. Clearly, polarization with Beijing is not a desirable thing to do at this time and in this situation. In 1998 when the Anglican Church in Hong Kong elevated their diocese into an independent province within the universal Anglican Communion, they wanted to make it clear that they were no longer under the jurisdiction of the mother church in England (14). As discussed earlier in this chapter, the Vatican must find a solution to the present impasse with Beijing, for the good of the Church in China. This can be done either by setting up a "Chinese Rite", or by internal reform of the Roman Curia particularly pertaining to the appointment of Bishops. (14)

CHAPTER V

INCULTURATION

End Notes

1. Enculturation, according to Margaret Mead, is "the process of learning a culture in all its uniqueness and particularity." See, *Current Anthropology*, 1963, Vol. 4, p. 187.
2. C.R. Beazley. *Prince Henry the Navigator*. New York: Prentice-Hall, 1904, pp. 56-58. Also, the writer of this book was born and raised in Macao where Matteo Ricci first lived before entering China, and personally witnessed some of these manifestations.
3. *1 Peter* 2:9 and *Exodus* 19:6.
4. *Acts of the Apostles* 15: 1-31
5. For biographical information on Francis Xavier, consult James Brokerick, S.J. *Saint Francis Xavier*. New York: Doubleday, 1952 and his other work: *The Origins of the Jesuits* (New York, Doubleday, 1960).
6. The Jesuit policy of accommodation was discussed in the work by George Elison, *Deus Destroyed: the image of Christianity in Early Modern Japan*. Cambridge, Mass.: Harvard University Press, 1973.
7. H.J. Coleridge (ed.), *The Life and Letters of St. Francis Xavier*, (London, 1902) vol. 1, p. 58-60. Also, John D. Young. Confucianism and Christianity: the First Encounter. Hong Kong: The University Press, 1983, p. 14.
8. George Harris, "The Mission of Matteo Ricci, S.J.: A Case Study of an Effort at Guided Cultural Change in China in the Sixteenth Century", *Monumenta Serica XXV* (1966), p. 56; also quoted in John D. Young, op. cit., p.23.

9. "Church must help preserve Chinese wisdom", Western Catholic Reporter, 2008 Oct 20, p. 1.
10. Eliza Morrison, Memoirs of the Life and Labour of Robert Morrison (London: Orme, Brown, Green and Longmans, 1989, vol. 2.)

11. Edmond Tang, "The Catholic Church in the Peoples Republic of China", (updated by Jerome Heyndrickx), *Pro Mundi Vita Studies*, No. 15, June 1990, p. 20.
12. For a complete text of his address, see Church and State Relations in China: Characteristics and Trends, Tripod, XV (88), pp. 5-18.
13. Cf. "A Small Boat on the Boundless Ocean - The Future of the Catholic Church in Mainland China." A presentation published in the Yi China Message, and reprinted in the Sedos Bulletin (Rome), vol. 27 no.4, April 15, 1995.
14. For more detailed discussion on this topic, see: Maria G. Lau, "Towards a Theology of the Local Church," Unpublished Ph.D. Thesis, University of Louven, 1989.

CHAPTER VI

EPISODES OF THE FAILURE OF EUROPEAN CHRISTIANITY TO TAKE ROOT IN CHINA

86 A.D. to 1,500 AD

We recall in Chapter IV that the first phase of historic Christianity in China involved the Nestorians and the Franciscans. These early missionaries did not preach the gospel in the context of the Chinese culture. They were a kind of contemporary chaplain looking mainly after the spiritual needs of the merchants and the nobility in the imperial courts. Only incidentally were they preaching the gospel among some of the local population who showed curiosity about the new religion. Furthermore, they did not prepare local missionaries for continuing the task. With time and unsettled political conditions these "imported" missionaries died out one by one and there was no one to replace them.

Nestorianism was Syrian-Persian Christianity. It stayed in China for a brief period and disappeared when it came under persecution. In 635, a learned Nestorian monk (Alopen) arrived with his followers at Xian, Capital City of the western province during the Tang dynasty. Tang was the most prosperous dynasty in Chinese history, not only politically, militarily and economically, but also in terms of learning. Emperor T'ai Tsung was a tolerant person and eager to learn. He received the Nestorian monks with great honour, and decreed that these religious men be given their "temples" and living quarters.

The Nestorian Church came at a time when Buddhism was beginning to have an influence on Chinese society after three learned Chinese monks were able to venture to India over difficult terrains, and brought back a great number of the holy books to Xian, the cultural capital of China at that time. As the Nestorian priests used Buddhist terms in the translation of the scriptures, they were therefore regarded as a Buddhist sect. Unfortunately they were included later in the Buddhist persecution. Since the Nestorians borrowed too much from the Buddhist tradition which was not fundamentally Chinese, Nestorianism was not able to take root in Chinese soil. It existed for a brief period, but disappeared gradually after the persecution.

However, eight hundred years later, it surfaced again in China at the beginning of the Yuen Dynasty (1260 – 1368) when China came under the Mongol rule. The mother of Kublai Khan, the emperor, was a Nestorian. Members of the Nestorian Church in China consisted mainly of Mongol nobles and Persians who came to China for trade. Its circle of influence was therefore very restricted. It survived only for a brief period. Gradually it faded away with the decline of the Mongol rule.

In 1275 Marco Polo arrived in China with his father and uncle. This paved the way for the second phase of historic Christianity in China. Two Dominicans accompanied them during the first part of their journey. Unfortunately these two priests were not able to reach China; they had to return to Italy half way through this difficult journey. The trip was very dangerous. There were robbers and undisciplined soldiers all along the way.

Emperor Kublai Khan of the Yuen Dynasty warmly received them and was impressed by their background. On their departure, Kublai Khan asked them to see the Pope when they got home. He would like the Pope to send missionaries to China.

Thus the second phase of the history of Christianity in China began when in 1294 Franciscan archbishop John of Montecorvino arrived in Beijing. In less than five years he was able to build a church in Beijing, and by 1305 he already had more than 6000 baptized followers. In 1313, Rome sent six more Franciscans to assist John. Three of them died on the way. The other three were able to survive the dangerous trip and eventually arrived in Beijing. One of them, Andrew of Perugia, was assigned to the coastal province of Fujian (1).

Unfortunately, Archbishop John of Montecorvino did not have a successor when he died. History seems to indicate that the Pope appointed a few other bishops to come to China, but they never arrived. Over the years without leadership, and eventually without the support and protection of the Mongols as the Yuen Dynasty was collapsing, the Church gradually died out in China (2). That was the situation until three hundred years later in 1583 when Matteo Ricci, an Italian Jesuit, reintroduced Christianity to China.

History has clearly pointed out that a church that depended solely for its survival on the participation and support of an elite group of people such as royalties in the imperial court would not be able to survive. It must take root in the culture of the masses to endure the test of time.

CHRISTIANITY UNDER THE JESUIT POLICY OF ACCOMMODATION:

1583-1742

As a Jesuit, Matteo Ricci followed his Order's guidelines for cultural accommodation (3). In addition to adopting the local language, social customs and manners, he went further and initiated intellectual exchange of scientific, philosophical and theological ideas, resulting in a syncretism of East-West cultures. He demonstrated clear evidence that Confucianism and Christianity are not diametrically opposed to each other. In many instances, they can even be compatible. (4) Thus, in Christianizing Confucianism, Ricci had won a respectable place for Christianity in Chinese society, at a time when both Europe and China were experiencing a renaissance of their own.

Matteo Ricci's evangelization process anticipated teachings of *Nostra Aetate* of 1965 and other post-conciliar Church documents such as *Gaudium et Spes, Ecclesiam Suam* and *Evangelii Nuntiandi,* — all of which encourage a spirit of dialogue and proclamation — 400 hundred years before the publication of these documents! Can we not call him a visionary of his time?

How far could Ricci go in his effort of cultural accommodation without coming into conflict with Christian theology? The Chinese Rites issue was the biggest stumbling block.

The Problem of Ancestral Worship

The English philosopher Herbert Spencer considered the ancestor cult to be the root of every religion, and many scholars agreed with him in the sense that the veneration of ancestors maintained the authority of the elders, social control and traditional attitude (5). A belief in survival after death was also widespread among Indo-European peoples from as early as Palaeolithic and Neolithic periods (6). In fact, the practice of filial piety towards parents was deeply rooted in patriarchal religions among the Hebrews, Greeks, Romans and the Chinese. The Christian belief in resurrection had provided a good foundation for remembering the dead, although often they expressed such veneration in churches as opposed to the Chinese who did so within their families and clans (7).

In Christianity, prayers and sacrifices to the dead are seen as a violation of the First Commandment, but prayers **for** the dead are theologically permissible. The Christian position permits veneration of the ancestors, including prayers and liturgy, but not to the extent found in the ancestor cult. The Council of Trent justifiably defended such veneration after the Reformation.

Many scholars agreed that in China, ancestral veneration had degenerated into ancestral worship, particularly in its exterior form resulting from centuries of syncretism of Taoism, Buddhism and Shamanism. In its early stages in Confucius' time, people remembered their ancestors in veneration, and all the Classics point out that Confucius himself worshipped Shang-ti or the Lord of Heaven, but refuted the existence of other spirits. In fact the *Book of Rites* (8) taught that everything on earth had its roots in Heaven, and all persons were rooted in their ancestors. The purpose of the Annual Veneration outside the capital was for all, particularly the kings, to remember their roots.

To this day, Chinese Ancestor Worship has the following important meaning (9)

(a) Affirmation of one's roots (From whom did I come?). It is therefore important that ancestors must be remembered on New Year's, at the wedding ceremony, and so on.

(b) The idea of immortality. (The spirit of the ancestor is present within the family among his or her children. They become like guardian angels to protect their posterity).

(c) Participation of the living with the ancestors' spirit during worship, so that when it is one's turn to leave this world, one will join the rank and file of one's ancestors.

Ricci and the Jesuits had the difficult task of deciding if this practice of Ancestor Worship was veneration or worshipping of the ancestors. Eventually, after studying all the Classics, Ricci decided that Chinese ancestor worship was indeed veneration, and not worship of the dead. They began to compromise by allowing the baptized Chinese to continue the practice.

By so doing, the Jesuits met with strong opposition in their accommodation effort, not from the Chinese, but from other missionary groups such as the Dominicans and the Franciscans, who had later followed the Jesuits to preach the Gospels in China. Their rivals denounced the Jesuits in Rome. To resolve this issue, the Jesuits had asked Emperor Kangxi's opinion. The Emperor was not a Chinese himself; he was a Manchu. However, after lots of input by his court scholars, he agreed with the Jesuits. He even wrote a personal letter to the Pope to state his position. When the Emperor's letter reached Rome, endless disputes took place in the Sacred Congregation for the Doctrine of the Faith. The conflict soon developed into a political issue with debates all over Europe. (10)

Finally, the Jesuits received a fatal blow from Rome. Pope Clement XI in 1704 forbade any Chinese Christians to venerate their ancestors and Confucius. Within the reality of Chinese culture, this command actually meant that to remain a Christian, one had to cease to be a Chinese. Thus, the emperor was greatly offended when the Papal visitor, Maillard de Tournon, arrived in Beijing on April 2, 1705, bringing with him the viewpoint of Rome. The emperor therefore decreed the following after seeing the Papal visitor:

No one [of the Vatican delegates] can read Chinese books, but they preach a lot of doctrine. This is really laughable. How can they presume to speak about Chinese customs and ceremonies?...From now on it is not necessary for Westerners to engage in religious activity in China, and we forbid it (11).

In response to the Papal Edict which forbade 'ancestor worship', China started persecuting all Christians in the Middle Kingdom. We must not overlook the fact that in Imperial China, the emperor was both the head of state and head of the religion like the pope. Rome must have found it difficult to accept the ruling on the Rites issue from the emperor, since the Pope was the head of the Catholic Church. This is the first time the Church in China was caught in a conflict with authorities: both the pope and the Chinese Emperor wanted to uphold their respective power and authority.

Historian Malcolm Hay asks these questions:

...Why did an enterprise, so sensible, so simple, and obviously conducive to the unity and peace of the whole world, so utterly fail that the memory of it and the ideal by which it was inspired have been completely forgotten? ...It was wrecked, not by any intrinsic faults of its own, but by unfortunate rivalries between Jesuits and other Roman Catholic... missionary orders, which had nothing to do with Christianity or China or India. (12)

Indeed such failure was recognized and lamented by other historians including Otto Karrer who sadly commented on the episode as follows:

The last attempt on a wide scale to take account of the native mind was made in the Far East by the Jesuit missionaries in the 17th century. It failed... The decision in the controversy of the Chinese Rites destroyed the Far Eastern mission which began so auspiciously (13)

Today the Catholic Church has accepted and allowed Ancestral Veneration among the Asians when it is considered a cultural ritual and not a religious one. It is parallel to the Catholic teaching of the Communion of the Saints. On the contrary, many of the Protestant denominations still consider this cultural event as contradicting the Christian teaching, and hence have aroused opposition from those Chinese who still hold on to their traditional culture. Perhaps this can explain why Christians remain a minority in the vast Chinese population.

CHRISTIANITY FOLLOWED THE STEPS OF WESTERN IMPERIALISM: 1842-1949

Since then, for almost two hundred years, Christianity was totally wiped out of China until 1842, when Britain defeated China in the infamous Opium War. Christian missions became part of imperialism and colonialism in China, contrary to the effort of Ricci and the Jesuit mission who presented Christianity to the Chinese with respect and peace.

As a result of the defeat in 1842, China was forced to sign the "Nanjing Treaty," an unequal treaty imposed by Western colonial powers. The Treaty did not explicitly give privileges to the Church but it included the "Extraterritoriality," a judicial system in which Western persons who had committed crimes in China would not be subject to Chinese law (14). Western missionaries were protected by such law, and were able to function freely in China, to the extent that they would not give any consideration to any aspects of Chinese culture. The situation kindled Chinese hatred toward Westerners in general, and the Church — including the missionaries — in particular. Later more unequal treaties were signed aimed at giving protection to missionaries in China.

As foreign dominance increased, in 1846 the Manchurian Court in China reluctantly nullified the prosecution against Christian missionaries — a prohibition started two hundred years before as a result of the Rites issue. But the anti-foreign sentiment had increased so much that the Chinese clergy found it very difficult to assume church leadership under foreign bishops. In Rome the Congregation for the Propagation of the Faith proposed a local church hierarchy to the European bishops in China. The bishops concluded the following:

> ...a European missionary only needed two thirds of the ballots cast to be chosen as candidate for bishop... a Chinese priest was ...required to receive more than two thirds of the ballots in order to be chosen, he also had to obtain all of the votes of the European missionaries taking part in the election (15).

Clearly the European bishops did not want to see a Chinese elected as Bishop. From the above conclusion which they submitted to Rome, any foreign missionary could "veto" any Chinese who would be chosen. The first effort by Rome to indigenize the Church in China failed.

Protestant Evangelism

Compared to Rome's effort to indigenize the local clerical hierarchy, Protestant missionaries, in their effort to convey the Christian message, were more inclined to confront Chinese civilization rather than to accommodate it. (16) One Protestant missionary wrote, "...under the outward show of politeness and refinement imparted to the educated Chinese chiefly by Confucianism, there is almost nothing but cunning, ignorance, rudeness, vulgarity, arrogant assumption and inveterate hatred of everything foreign." (17) As a matter of fact, missionaries in the 19th century generally considered non-western cultures as heretical and incongruous with Christianity, and therefore rejected them. Some missionaries even went to the extent of preventing the Chinese cultures from contaminating the children of believers and felt the responsibility of educating them in the Western tradition. (18). In short, many missionaries looked down on the Chinese ethics, thought and ways of living and aimed at reforming the culture. Consequently the missionary schools followed a westernized system without including any study of the Chinese classics. Hence their endeavors in general failed to meet the needs of the society. Thus, in the minds of the Chinese, Christianity and Western culture were just two sides of the same coin. Had European missionaries understood Confucianism, they would realize that Confucianism demands human efforts (i.e. self-cultivation) for anyone to become righteous, while Christian virtue was dependent upon the spirit (i.e. Grace). (19) Indeed, European missionaries had not studied the Chinese culture well enough to understand that there are many similarities between Christian teachings and Confucius ethics.

By giving protection to the missionaries, the unequal treaties had unintentionally implicated the Church in the foreign oppression in China. Consequently the Church became a scapegoat for the agitated anger of the Chinese populace. Moreover, a great number of Western missionaries were behaving arrogantly and domineeringly at that time, creating misunderstandings between the converts and the "atheists." For example, if a Chinese Catholic got into a dispute over any matter with his fellow countrymen, the Western missionaries would rush to his rescue. The intention of the Western powers to dominate China was made clear, when in 1875, the Qing government sought to establish diplomatic relations with the Vatican, and the French government objected (20). The Boxer Rebellion in the late 19th Century in China, in fact, was a cultural reaction to the ignorance of the Chinese culture by the European missionaries who aligned with their respective governments to make inroads in China.

As highly organized political and religious institutions, both the Catholic Church and Protestant Church were increasingly perceived as an accomplice of Western infiltration of China. In the early 1920s when the "May Fourth Movement" was in full swing to give China its own national and cultural identity by adopting "pragmatism" and Confucianism as the official state philosophy and religion, Christianity as a foreign religion became the adversary of this and subsequent movements of national awareness. (21)

The Christian Churches made one mistake after another especially in 1934, (three years before Japan started a full-scale invasion of China), when the Japanese government set up a puppet government in its recently occupied northeastern China. To the surprise of every Chinese, the Vatican recognized this government and appointed a nuncio to handle diplomatic matters. By doing so, the Vatican openly challenged China's sovereignty at a time when Chinese nationalism was reaching its peak. This act aroused hostility from both the Nationalist government and the Chinese people.

According to Paul Cohen who is an expert on the early Christian missions in China, "where the missionaries of the late nineteenth century were least successful" was in selling to the Chinese the proposition that Western learning and institutions, and the wealth and power that accompanied them, were somehow rooted in Christianity." (22)

Nevertheless, Christianity had prompted the educated elite in China to re-examine their cultural heritage and, as in the case of the late 19th century Chinese reformer Káng

Yu-wei, he advanced the idea that in accepting Christianity, the Chinese could realize that "they could reject God and still have progress." (23) In retrospect, the various movements of nationalism in the recent history of China have basically looked upon Christianity as a tool for modernization more than for its spiritual value.

Some missionaries, however, awoke to the importance of cultural accommodation, especially after the May 4 Movement in China following WWI when intellectuals and politicians began to look for a Chinese identity to reform the country. The Catholic Church began to examine once again the issue of cultural accommodation on November 1919 in the issuing of a new document, "Maximum Illud", and the appointment of an Apostolic Delegate, Mgr. Celso Constantini to build an indigenous Church in China free from any previous imperial political influences. As Religious Orders (Societies) were given the task of evangelization by Rome, the Franciscans were very successful in following the new direction from the Holy See to preach the Christian message, particularly in hamlets and towns of rural China. (24)

During this period, the general approach taken by both the Catholic Church and Protestant Church in evangelism was by responding to the Chinese social needs in providing education and social services, such as schools, universities, hospitals or homes for the aged. This is known as "Indirect Evangelism".

We can see that when evangelism followed the steps of colonialism and not by peaceful means, it would not be sustainable by itself. It did not get the right soil to nourish its growth. It withered away with time.

CHRISTIANITY AT THE BRINK OF BEING WIPED OUT: 1949 to 1978

The establishment of the People's Republic of China in 1949 began not only the communist rule in China, but also the worst relationship between the State and the Church. The communist government lumped the Church and the Western imperial powers together as one. The Western nations were supporting the Nationalist government now in exile in Taiwan, and since these nations were either Catholic or Protestant, all Christian churches were labeled as accomplices, and were to suffer in the ensuing years.

After the success of the communist takeover, China became an atheistic state. The communist government sought to strengthen its power in order to bring about a new political order by excluding all foreign influences. The hostility of the government towards the church as both a political and religious institute is understandable. Furthermore, the Catholic Church's "imperialistic" image as an ally of Western powers, its relations with the Nationalist government in exile in Taiwan, and its wealth and influence in world politics had certainly caused the new government to be very suspicious of the Vatican. No wonder that the communists considered the Vatican as a "wolf in a sheep's clothing" in all its propaganda.

With China's involvement in the Korean War, Beijing began persecuting all Christian churches. It expelled all foreign missionaries, and encouraged both the Catholic and Protestant Churches to become independent and autonomous of their foreign mother institutions. Thus the "Three Self Movement" churches came into being. Both the Catholic Church and Protestant Church had to be self-supporting, self-administrating, and self-propagating. Those who resisted this independent church movement were given jail sentences. Bishop Ignatius Gong Pinmei of Shanghai and Bishop Dominic Deng Yiming of Guangzhou were given indefinite jail terms, as were a great number of loyal followers.

Uncooperative Protestant church leaders and followers, too, met the same fate as the Catholics.

The Church further suffered during the Chinese Cultural Revolution from 1966 to 1977, when the ruthless young Red Guards burned down church buildings, and persecuted church leaders and followers. Under severe mental depression, many of them committed suicide.

CHAPTER VI

EPISODES OF THE FAILURE OF EUROPIAN CHRISTIANITY TO TAKE ROOT IN CHINA

End Notes

1. See *Truth Monthly*, March 2000, p. 14 (Chinese Evangelical, Vancouver, Canada).
2. Zhao Quingyuan. A Chronology of the Chinese Dioceses in Their Successive Bishops. Taiwan: Window Press, 1980.
3. The Jesuits were well known for their cultural accommodation methods, contrary to the Portuguese and Spanish who insisted that Christianity in missionary lands should not be adulterated by native culture.
4. Young, John D. *East-West Synthesis: Matteo Ricci and Confucianism*. Hong Kong: Centre of Asian Studies, University of Hong Kong, 1980, p. iii-iv.
5. Kung, Hans and Julia Ching., *Christianity and Chinese Religions*. Toronto: Doubleday, 1989, p. 37.
6. Eliade, Mircea (n.d.). *A History of Religious Ideas*. Chicago: The University Press, p. 9.
7. Kung, *op. cit.*, p.37
8. For an English translation of the Book of Rites, one of Confucius Classics, see James Legg, *The Four Books*. Taipei: Culture Books.
9. Ho, Louis Kam-tat. *Theological and Cultural Accommodation: Matteo Ricci and the Jesuit Mission in China*. Unpublished Master of Theological Studies thesis. Edmonton, Canada: St. Stephen's College, 1996.
10. Kung, *op. sit.* 241.
11. Fang Hao. *A History of Interrelations Between China and the West*, 5 vols. Taipei: Chinese Cultural Press, 1959. pp. 160-165.
12. Hay, Malcolm. *Failure in the Far East: Why and How the Breach Between the Western World and China First Began*. Belgium: Wetteren, 1956, p. 1.

13. Sebes, Joseph S.J. *A Bridge Between East and West: Father Matteo Ricci, S.J., His Times, His life, and His Methods of Cultural Accommodation.* Rome: Historical Institute of the Society of Jesus, 1978, p. 10.
14. Beers, Burton F., *World History: Patterns of Civilization.* Scarborough, Ontario: Prentice Hall Canada Inc., 1989, pp. 167-168.
15. Wei, Qingxin. *French Policy Towards Missionary Work* in China. Translated by Huang Qinghua. Beijing: The Chinese Academy of Sciences, 1991, p. 6.
16. John D. Young, "Resurrecting 'Chinese Culture': Historical Perspectives on Christianity in China", in *Christianity in China: Foundations for Dialogue.* Hong Kong: Centre of Asian Studies, University of Hong Kong, 1993., p.5-17.
17. Paul Cohen, *China and Christianity*, p. 80. Quoted by John D. Young, ibid., p.7.
18. Cf. R. Lechler, "on the Relation of Protestant Missions to Education", *Records of Conference 1877*, pp. 164-6.
19. John D. Young, *op. cit.*
20. Lam, Anthony S.K. *The Catholic Church in Present Day China: Through Darkness and Light.* English Edition. Hong Kong: The Holy Spirit Study Centre, 1997, pp. 49-81.
21. Lam, *ibid.*
22. Paul Cohen, "Christian missions", in *Cambridge History of China*, pp. 588-9.
23. Paul Cohen, Ibid.
24. Dominic Gandolfi, "Franciscan Missions in China (1920-1950): Challenge and Responses," in Beatrice Leung and John D. Young, *Christianity in China: Foundations for Dialogue.* Hong Kong: Centre of Asian Studies, University of Hong Kong, 1993.

CHAPTER VII

THE DEVOPMENT OF AN INDIGENOUS CHRISTIAN CHURCH SINCE 1978

The recovery of the Chinese church took place when the Eleventh Central Committee of the Chinese Communist Party convened in Beijing in December 1978. The Committee adopted an open reform policy for the government to implement, including rehabilitation of religious institutes and organizations. Both the Protestant and Catholic Churches were again recognized. Two prominent leaders from both the Catholic Church and the Protestant Church were appointed to be delegates to the Chinese People's Political Consultative Conference in Beijing in 1978. The government promised to compensate both Churches for the loss and damage of property during the Cultural Revolution. But by then the division within each Church had become obvious. Two divisions came to the surface: the Official Church and the House Church for the Protestant; the Open Church and Underground Church for the Catholic.

In the previous chapters we discussed the government Religious Policy known as the Three Self Movement. The Three Self Movement refers to the self-administration, self-support and self-propagation. In sum, this policy aims at fostering independence and local development of churches away from foreign influence and control. It has its origin from the movement of anti-imperialism in China during the Korean War (1950-54). When the Korean War started, it was hardly one year since the Communists took over China, and the country as a whole was devastated by both long years of Japanese invasion and internal strife. Yet it took China just overnight to decide on participating in the Korean War. For the first time in world history, China as a third world country dared to challenge the most powerful nation of the western world, the United States of America.

Under the prevailing political tension, all foreign missionaries were considered spies and dangerous elements of subversion, and were ordered to leave the country immediately. Church properties were confiscated. The government demanded that all Christian churches, Protestant and Catholic alike, sever their ties from their foreign mother institutions, including the Holy See, and to become completely independent of any outside support — financial or otherwise. After the example of Henry VIII of England in the 16th Century to establish the Church of England, China became the first sovereign nation in modern times, to set up two independent churches, one for the Protestants, and one for the Catholics.

The Roman Catholic Church

In the case of the Catholic Church, the government sponsored the establishment of the Chinese Catholic Patriotic Association (CCPA) which continues to develop as the liaison body between the government and the Bishop's Conference. Together, the CCPA (as the political wing) and the Conference of Bishops (the spiritual or religious body) govern the Official Catholic Church in China. The CCPA also organized the appointment and ordination of bishops without the consent of Rome. Those Catholics who chose to remain loyal to the Holy See and the universal church had no choice but to go underground.

Besides the Catholic Church, China does not seem to have problems of authority in dealing with other religious followers within its territory. For example, Buddhists, Muslims and Protestants do not have a centrally organized structure such as the Roman Catholic Church with a universal head. There is no problem of demanding undivided allegiance from them.

The present knotty issue of the Sino-Vatican relationship lies in the fact that both China and the Vatican, being two separate authorities, failed to compromise on two important issues. They are the "One China" political notion which requires the Vatican to move its embassy from Taipei to Beijing, and the Chinese demand for non-interference in its internal affairs by the Vatican, namely the appointment of bishops. From the Chinese position, these two issues infringe on national sovereignty. From the position of Rome, it is a loss of authority or unity. Thus the Catholic Church in China today is caught between being loyal to the nation first, or to the Pope as the head of the Church. The issue is further complicated when China views the Vatican as a political entity first, and spiritual leader second. Furthermore, in the eyes of the Chinese leadership, loyalty to the Pope by the Chinese Catholics poses a risk of national security as they refer to the previous pope John Paul II in bringing down the Polish Communist Government with the collaboration of the American CIA by the end of the 1980's.

In the previous chapters we understand that the conflict between the Vatican and Chinese authority is not new. In the Rites Controversy during the seventeenth century, Matteo Ricci and the Jesuit Mission considered the Chinese ritual reverence of ancestors comparable to the Catholic concept of communion of saints. Their position was backed by the Emperor but challenged by other missionary orders such as the Dominicans and the Franciscans. When Pope Clement XI condemned Chinese Ancestor Worship as heretical, and forbade any Chinese Catholic to practice it, Emperor Kangxi was offended. He ordered the persecution of all Catholics in China. It was a conflict of authorities because the leaders of both sides considered themselves head of the church (1).

Such Sino-Vatican conflict has caused suffering and confusion in the Chinese Catholic Church. We often hear reports of the persecution of the members of the "Underground Church", poor quality of priest formation or training, chaos in spiritual leadership, confusion among lay Catholics concerning the underground or the official church, and puzzlement over the future of the Chinese Catholic Church in general. On the other hand, we hear reports that the number of Catholics in China has increased to 12 million from 8 million in 1988, and the number keeps growing. (2) Indeed, as the president of the Conference of Chinese Catholic Patriotic Association points out, now is the golden age for Christian evangelization of China. (3) The ground is in fact very fertile, but how will the Vatican sow the seeds of the gospel?

The long-standing dispute between the Vatican and China is in no one's best interest. It is possible for China and the Vatican to come to terms with each other, if both sides show the good will and make the appropriate compromise. As the old saying goes, "if there is a will, there is a way". The *South China Morning Post* (4) in Hong Kong described the situation this way: "We can trace the split to its roots in the early Chinese radicalism in 1949 and the right-wing traditions of the church, which preached poverty while enjoying the largesse of dictators."

The *South China Morning Post* goes on to say that "It is evident from the preceding account that any breakthrough in Sino-Vatican relationship hinges on matters that are more than spiritual. The issues at stake have more serious implications than do fine points of theology." To be more explicit, the matter touches on the conflict of authorities between church unity and reforms for both China and the Vatican.

The Underground Catholic Church

In the previous Chapter, we briefly touched on the Underground Church. Communities of the Underground Church are usually located in Northern China, particularly the rural areas. They emerged in the late seventies and grew rather fast during the eighties but recently have become undefined. The regions where they concentrate have a long history of European evangelization, particularly by the French missionaries. The people in those regions generally display a conservative and inward looking attitude, in contrast to the southern, especially coastal regions where people are more adaptive and outward looking.

These underground church communities would not accept the leadership of the Open Church and consider it as the puppet of the government. As well, they consider the Open Church not authentic Catholic because it is not a part of the Universal Church. They refuse to cooperate with the government and maintain loyalty to the Pope; hence they are constantly being persecuted by the government for unlawful religious gatherings.

The handling of the Underground Church by government officials varies from place to place according to the particular local authorities. As the Chinese society began to be more open, the government was at first tolerant of the activities of the Underground Church communities. Many communist cadres were impressed by the dedication, if not holiness, of the Underground Church priests, because they had witnessed their faith when they were in jail or labour camps during the Cultural Revolution. Later, as the government began to formulate new religious policies, it started to persecute both the clerics and the laity of the Underground

Church members. The government has repeatedly stated that the most urgent need in China is social stability, and organized religions, especially when they are affiliated with foreign political authorities, are considered political and social threats to a united China. In fact, late 19th century history of China has good examples of organized religious groups that attempted to subvert the government. The outstanding case was the White Lotus Church combining Christianity with folk religion to overthrow the Qing Dynasty Government, without complete success. (5)

In the eyes of the Chinese government, the Vatican is always considered a political entity first, and a religious organization second. It is fully conscious of the role played by the Vatican in the communist downfall in Poland at the end of the 1980s. The government has repeatedly warned Underground Church members that they must register with the Religious Affairs Bureau to be accepted legally; failing to do so will result in their arrests by the Public Security Bureau. Many devout Catholic clergy and laity believe that if they join the Open Church, their salvation is at stake as the Open Church is not an authentic Catholic Church. In my view, this is gross ignorance.

Recently Rome has urged the Underground and the Open Churches to reconcile with each other for the sake of unity. As Chinese society becomes more and more open, and with more visits and contacts between the universal and the Chinese Church, many Underground Church members have slowly but steadily participated in the Open Church.

It all depends on the regions where they are located. The division appears to be going away along the coast and in the cities where the Open Church predominates. However, in the interior the Underground Church is strong, with a large membership.

The Underground Church has caused a bad image for the Chinese leadership. By constantly persecuting the

Underground Church, the Chinese government has brought upon itself international condemnation for violating human rights, and therefore strong embarrassment in the international community.

The hostility, accusation and attack between these two Churches over the issue of Church legitimacy have sapped a large portion of the energy of each Church. Coupled with government persecution of the Underground Church and state control of the Open Church, there is little each Church can do for evangelical and pastoral effort.

Both the previous pope John Paul II and the current pope Benedict XVI have urged both churches to come to reconciliation. The Holy See is to a great extent responsible for this internal church schism. Back in the 1980's, Pope John Paul II conferred "Special Faculties" to the underground bishops. By such special privilege, the Underground Church bishops were allowed to ordain new priests and bishops as they thought fit, without having to obtain permission from the Holy See. By so doing, the Underground Church would have a continuous supply of leadership. To avoid further split within the Church in China, in his pastoral letter to the Church in China in 2007, Pope Benedict XVI took back this special privilege, hoping that this two factions would merge soon. (6)

At the end of 2008 when this book was being prepared there was no sign of these two factions coming back together quickly, but there were indications of a slow merging. In this hoped for merge, a number of issues would have to be settled, such as the status of the Underground Church bishops and priests and the redrawing of the parish boundaries. Hope is there as the nation becomes more and more open to the outside world.

The Protestant Church

There are no Protestant denominations in China. All previous denominations have been grouped together under one church, the Chinese Patriotic Christian Church. Theological differences were compromised by various denominations by using the Evangelical model and the Bible as the frame of reference. Like the split in the Catholic Church, the Protestant Church in China consists of the Official Church (or Lianhui in Chinese) and the House Church. The Official Church with government recognition is under the jurisdiction of the Three-Self Patriotic Association and the Christian Council, but the House Church is unrecognized by the government. It has unrelated member units or communities all over the country, particularly in areas away from the major population centers.

The growth of Protestant Christians is much greater than the Catholics, and is indeed a unique ecclesiastical phenomenon since China's adoption of the Open Door Policy in 1978. Today in China, for every Catholic Christian there are more than three Protestant Christians.

As the Protestant Official Church is not under the jurisdiction of a foreign church hierarchy such as the Roman Catholic, it has harmonized well with the government policy of the "Three Self Movement", much better than the Catholic Open (Official) Church. This, perhaps, explains in part why it has grown so rapidly. Its head, the Right Reverent Bishop Ding Quon-fen, is well respected and accepted both inside and outside China by the Christian communities. He is often invited to officiate at church events in Hong Kong and Macao, and sometimes overseas. (7)

The Protestant House Church

The Protestant House Church mirrors, in many ways, the early church movement in the Apostolic Time. Most of the House Church communities refuse to register with the Official Church, and are constantly being harassed or persecuted by the local authorities for illegal religious or subversive activities. The persecution can take the form of either prison sentence or re-education through labor. Heavy fines are also common. The Protestant House Church communities are dissatisfied with the Official Church in becoming a corrupt agent of the government, and they want the freedom to proclaim the gospel or hold worship services at a believer's household. Some communities are just small Christian community movements for biblical studies and liturgical celebrations of hymn singing, while others may have an extensive and even elaborate organization structure such as having printing and seminary facilities. Some are conservative in doctrine, and others may have cult characteristics. Some may register with a local official church, but others may completely ignore any government regulations for religious gathering.

These groups can often be identified with the following characteristics. As a whole, they are dynamic in faith, eager to preach the gospel to anyone coming across their path, and fundamental in theological understanding. As well, they are devout in religious practice, informal in liturgical rituals, willing to form new communities, and flexible in organization. Usually the leaders are charismatic, but have little training in theology. When we read about persecution of Christians in China, it is about these clandestine Christian House Communities who are antagonistic to the Official Church and the Government. European and North American evangelical or missionary societies have been trying to give them both material and spiritual support, but in doing so they indirectly jeopardize their existence, and cause them trouble with the law, as the religious policy of China is based on the Three Self Movement which we already discussed earlier. Many are of the opinion that if they are left alone, they will grow better and become truly indigenous church communities with "Chinese Characteristics", a quality very much favored by the Chinese Authorities. Many theologians are of the opinion that their growth will lead to a Christianity that will genuinely take root in Chinese soil.

Like the Catholic Underground Church communities, the Protestant House Church communities are illegal by government standard, but they multiply fast in all rural, particularly remote, areas of China. As we mentioned earlier, their growth is due to the fact that they do not need an ordained leader to conduct their activities. When one lay leader gets into trouble with the government, another lay leader takes over. They do not celebrate the Sacraments as the Catholic counterparts do, but their focus on the Gospel gives them even stronger energy and zeal in evangelism unparalleled among other religions in China. When times are bad they seem to have all disappeared, but when the situation becomes favorable they resurface again to hold and participate in religious activities. It was estimated that each small Christian community on the average has high double-digit converts per year, and the growth becomes significant.

Following the teaching of Matthew 18:30 "For where two or three come together in my name, there am I with them", they appear to prefer a non-institutional church, and oppose to any rigid form of organizational structure. They are not pleased with Official Church being too worldly, and its ministers living immoral lives including debauchery and personal dishonesty in church finance. They regard the official church ministers not spiritual enough and not diligent enough when they only conduct liturgical services only once a week. Their religious conviction often transforms them from desperation into hope with faith and love in dealing with their own lives and those of their family members. Their concern of the End Time keeps them in constant vigilance to avoid immoral temptations and to keep the Christian purpose for living.

Some theologians wonder if this House Church is a genuine expression of Christian faith in a rather unique cultural context in contemporary China, or will some of communities deteriorate into isolated religious cults as they deviate from authentic Christian teachings and practices, such as the Waco Cult in the United States. This thinking is one of the reasons why the Chinese Authorities believe that the State must be able to supervise all religious activities to protect the well-being of its citizens.

In the next chapter we will examine the religious policy of China in order to formulate an idea about the future of Christianity in China.

CHAPTER VII

THE DEVELOPMENT OF INDIGENOUS CHRISTIAN CHURCH IN CHINA SINCE 1978

End Notes

1. For more information about this issue, please consult, Ho, Louis Kam-tat.Torn Between Authorities: A phenomenological Study of the Catholic Church in China Today. Unpublished Doctor of Ministry Dissertation. Edmonton, Canada: St. Stephen's College, 2002, pp. 144-146.
2. The official figure is 5,300,000. See, "Estimated Statistics for China's Catholic Church" (December 2007), *Tripod*, Winter 2007, p. 46.
3. K*ung Kao Po*, 1999 Feb. 28, p. A6; *World Journal*, 2008 Nov. 8, p.A7.
4. *South China Morning Post*, 1986 June 06, p.9.
5. Cf. John K. Fairbanks, *The Cambridge History of China*, vol. 10: Late Ch'íng, 1800-1911, Part 1. Cambridge, Mass.: Harvard University Press, 1974. (Under "Heavenly Peace Rebellion").
6. For details of the pastoral letter of Pope Benedict XVI to the Church in China, please go to the Appendix at the end of this book.
7. Both are the two Special Autonomous Regions of China continuing to maintain its previous colonial economic, social and judicial life or system except defense and foreign relations.

CHAPTER VIII

THE CURRENT RELIGIOUS POLICY OF CHINA RELATING TO CHRISTIANITY

To understand the church situation in China and to envision the future, we need to know the current religious policy of the Chinese Communist Government.
 We frequently read western media's reports on religious persecution in China. The Chinese media, however, report such incidents as criminal activities of certain religious members. Among the many questions that are raised about this issue I would include the following:

- Is there religious freedom in China today? If so how is it guaranteed?
- Does China have a policy about religion? If the answer is yes, what is the ideology underlying such policy?
- How is a policy of religion implemented in China? On the one hand, media reports often suggest that religion is booming in China; on the other hand there are frequent reports of religious persecutions. Can such ambiguity be explained?

To understand these questions, we have to trace the religious development in China since the communist take-over in 1949. We will come back to the above questions before we close this chapter (1).

As a communist state, China has adopted the ideology of Marxism and Leninism in governing the country. According to such ideology, religion is the opiate of the people. (2) It is the opiate because in all class struggles, marginal people suffer under the oppression and the hurt of capitalists, and therefore need painkillers to take care of their wounds. Most people cannot afford to buy opium; they take religion as a substitute to heal their wounds and to give them strength to go on living.

Throughout its history, China is well known for accommodating foreign beliefs to make something new of its own. The best example is Zen Buddhism, which is very Chinese in characteristic after two thousand years of development. In politics, Mao Zedong attempted something along the same line. He gave a Chinese appearance to Marxism and Leninism by incorporating them into his own work – the Thoughts of Mao Zedong or Maoism. Once the political philosophy became indigenous, he was able to change and adapt the ideology according the needs of the time or the situation.

As a communist state, China by definition must adopt an atheistic position. It perceives that churches often interfere or hinder government implementation of policies. However, when religion has become an integral part of the culture and life of the people, it is impossible for the government to eradicate it. Under persecution, religion will go underground and wait for the right time to germinate again. The compromise therefore, is for the government to use religion for definite purposes.

Former Premier Zhou Enlai (the outstanding Chinese diplomat and political architect) understood this well. He allowed churches to function when the People's Republic came into being in 1949. He stated that relations with the Vatican could be maintained if local churches would not collaborate with American imperialism and were loyal to the government. The Korean War began to change the scene when the Papal Nuncio Monsigor Antonio Riberi (together with a great number of foreign missionaries) was expelled from China.

In 1955 a turning point came about when the concept of church autonomy free from foreign control, commonly known as the "Three Self," or the "Three Self Movement" was fully implemented. This concept of "Three Self" referred to the church in China being able to be self-supporting, self-administrating and self-propagating. The resistance movement to this implementation, led by Bishop Ignatius Gong Pinmei in Shanghai and Bishop Dominic Deng Yiming in Guangzhou, as well as other Protestant leaders, was ruthlessly suppressed making way for the establishment of the "Chinese Catholic Patriotic Association" (CCPA) and the "Three Self Patriotic Association" for the Protestant Church in the middle of 1957. A number of Chinese policy analysts consider the Patriotic Association a smart manoeuvre by the Chinese authority, because it took away the argument of those who opposed the autonomous movement. The Protestants had fewer problems with this movement because they were not unified under one church authority such as the Catholics were under Rome. Although opposing Catholics could well argue that their resistance was a defense of the nature of their Catholic faith requiring communion with the Pope, they definitely had no ground for not joining the Catholic Patriotic Association to show love of their country. The Association elected patriotic priests to fill positions left vacant by those bishops who were expelled from China, and by those Chinese bishops who were put in jail because they resisted the new state direction for the Catholic Church.

Nevertheless, these patriotic priests were properly consecrated according to the teaching of Apostolic Succession. To this date the Holy See considers them valid but illicit bishops, because they were not installed according to the Canon Law of the Catholic Church. By 1962 there were already 42 illicit bishops serving various dioceses in China (3).

From the beginning of the Cultural Revolution in 1966 to the death of Mao in 1976, all religious manifestations disappeared. The Religious Bureau and the CCPA both ceased to function. The emergence of Deng Xiaoping as the new Chinese leader in 1978 began to change the religious scene. In this chapter, we will attempt to find out the rationale behind this change.

Religious Policy of Deng Xiaoping

Deng was educated in France, and he was aware of the contribution of religion to the western social fabric. Soon after his ascent to power, Deng introduced the "Four Modernizations" movement to reform the economy, agriculture, national defense, and science and technology. He adopted a new stance on the issue of church-state relationships. To bring about this change, he fully utilized the United Front to make positive use of religion for his economic reform. The slogan of the United Front was "seeking unity, preserving differences." This is an adaptation of Lenin's "One should unify the lesser enemy in order to struggle against the bigger enemy". Deng's focus was to rally all positive features and social strength to advance the reform movement, and in so doing the Chinese Communist Party (CCP) relaxed its ideological control at the Third Plenum of their Central Committee in December 1978. Such relaxation provided new breathing space for religious revival.

Factors Favoring Religious Development (4)

A number of events helped this religious revival to pick up momentum; soon after all religions started to expand rapidly. This acceleration of religious growth included all faiths, even folk religion. The major influencing factors include the following:

- The Cultural Revolution had eroded national confidence and trust in the CCP. People looked around for a new source of inspiration to fill their spiritual void. Communism ceased to be the "religion" for the masses. Soon after Mao's death, many writers expressed their disillusionment in the "Literature of the wounded," also known as the "Literature of the scared." This new literary expression fully depicted the suffering of the masses during the Cultural Revolution. Such popular resentment culminated in what is known as the first Tiananmen Incident of April 5, 1976 when younger people openly expressed that they were deceived by the communist party and fell victim to the power struggle of the political leaders. In addition, 13 years later on June 4, 1989 also at Tiananmen Square in Beijing, thousands of students staged an anti-corruption demonstration and demanded political reform. The government used the army to brutally suppress this "uprising," causing student deaths estimated in the thousands. This "massacre" further eroded people's faith in the communist party and the government.
- The reform movement caused a lapse of morality in most people. It was natural for them to ask what their suffering was for during the previous years under Mao. They began to take up the challenge of competition in all aspects of life when the government allowed the market economy to operate. Making

money replaced the ideal of service to the people. And with more money earned, they would pay little attention to the previously held moral code. People became pre-occupied with greed, and with greed came all kinds of social vice, including a decline in sexual morality. A review of Renmin Ribao (People's Daily) of March 3, 1982 and Sichuan Ribao (Sichuan Daily) of December 18, 1981 provides many stories of decadence at that time.
- An awakening of intellectual life and the easing of social policies also accompanied the reform movement. During this time, there was more scope for alternate views in philosophy and in religion to compensate the faith crisis in communism involving the weakening of party morale and credibility.

Relationship between Ideological Control and Religious Development

We can thus speculate that when there is less government ideological control, more religious freedom will build up. Seeing that it was impossible to totally suppress religion, the government came up with policies to make sure that religious developments would stay within the desired boundary and not become uncontrolled. Furthermore, such development should support the modernization effort, and conform to national interest and security, particularly the concern about foreign infiltration by means of religion.

Does this mean that religion will become an integral part of the government ideology? This is hardly the case. Former President Jiang Zemin and Premier Zhu Rongji, along with other high ranking government leaders, have repeatedly stated in their various speeches that China is an atheist state. They often refer to the idea of Karl Marx in *Document 19* (which is explained below) that when society is backward and poor, religion could contribute to social stability.

However as people become more educated and materially better off, religion would gradually lose its influence and might even disappear on its own. At this advanced stage of social development, religion becomes irrelevant, and can be eliminated without problem. Using physiology as an illustration in the context of Marxism, religion could be compared to the umbilical cord. As the fetus becomes fully mature and ready for birth, the umbilical cord loses its function. Therefore, Chinese leaders consider people with religious beliefs as part of society, and they should be involved in the modernization effort. However, they are not an integral part of governmental machinery, much as Jesus says in the Gospel that we are in the world but not of the world (*John* 17: 15-16).

Document 19 and the Religious Clause of the Chinese Constitution

On March 31, 1982 the Chinese Communist Party published *Document 19*. This is the basic text of the religious policy of Deng Xiaoping and became the foundation of Article 36 of the new Constitution as presented below. It articulates the government position on religion. "What is primary at the moment is the common goal of building a modernized powerful Socialist State, so the difference between believers and non-believers at this time is secondary."

Document 19 further points out that according to Marxism, it is a given that religion will naturally disappear when the people are sufficiently educated and understand the secrets of science. It is useless then to persecute religion as was done during the Cultural Revolution." *Document 19* provides the Party with both a long-term perspective, and present directives in dealing with religious issues by "neither turning a blind eye to it, nor mounting a frontal assault on the believers." *Document 19* also stresses the supervision of religious activities. It gives the government rationale for so doing, as explained earlier.

Article 36 of *The Constitution of the People's Republic of China* (promulgated for implementation on December 4, 1982) states the following about religious freedom:

> Citizens of the People's Republic of China enjoy freedom of religious belief.
>
> No state organ, public organization or individual may compel citizens to believe in, or not to believe in, any religion; nor may they discriminate against citizens who believe in, or do not believe in, any religion.
>
> The state protects normal religious activities. No one may make use of religion to engage in activities that disrupt public order, impair the health of citizens or interfere with the educational system of the state.
>
> Religious bodies and religious affairs are not subject to any foreign domination.

Other Important Statements or Documents Concerning Religion

Based on the above Article of the Constitution, the government has, since 1982, formulated several important documents and regional regulations to clarify the intent of the Article, such as the following taken from *Tripod,* (XIX (113), pp. 6-30):

- In September 1986, Jiang Ping, a Deputy Minister of the United Front and a leftist, presented his article in the official journal of the CCP *Hongqi*. His article is entitled *An Earnest Learning from the Religious Theory of Marxism and Religious Policy of the Party.*

In his presentation, he emphasizes again that religion is not compatible with China's ideology.

> It is true that religion has played positive roles in the development of world history, and revolutionaries and revolutionary groups have made successful use of religion. But our classic and famous Marxist dictum, "religion is the opium of the people", is still not out of date. It has been proved in both European and Chinese history that the negative role of religion can never be eliminated...After the liberation of our country...the religious situation changed considerably...To put it succinctly, the changes indicate that the religious organizations have changed only in appearance and political inclination, but they have not changed one iota in their social ideology (or world outlook) or their idealism...Religion is the complete opposite to atheism, so we cannot deny its anesthetic role in the social/ideological fields...We have no choice but to limit the degree and extent of religious activities.

- 1987: *Regulations on the Administrative Supervision of Religious Activities* was announced
- 1987: *Constitution of the Chinese Catholic Patriotic Association* was proclaimed
- December 5-10, 1990: Premier Li Peng delivered a speech at the National Conference on Religion. Li identified Christianity as one of the major elements among foreign enemy forces, out to subvert Communism and to divide and westernize China. Later, Jiang Zemin and other leaders repeatedly used

the main points of this speech in their own comments and remarks about religious freedom in China.

- January 1991: *Stipulations for the Villagers regarding Normal Catholic Church Activities* was made known. This was an internal document concerning a village in the Baoding District of the Hebei Province. It specified that "Everyone has the responsibility to struggle against the Catholic underground forces. Support and rewards will be given to those who daringly expose them...punishment will be meted out in accordance with the law to those who knew of the matter but did not report it and to those who masterminded the scheme."

- February 5, 1991: *Document No. 6: Some Problems concerning Further Improving Work on Religion* was declared. This internal document was the most important one after Document 19. It denounced the "Peaceful evolution" and foreign infiltration of Christianity. It gave Public Security agents complete power to make sure that no one used religion to endanger China's security. Following the spirit of this document, young priests were required to take part in a 3-month course on Marxism, Socialism, and the Religious Policy.

- 1994 January: former Premier Li Peng signed two political milestone documents to control and supervise religion. They were *Documents #144 and #145: Decrees of the State Council of the People's Republic of China.* Document 144 concerned the religious activities of foreigners and Document 145 discussed the supervision of religious venues.

- 1997 October 16: *The White Paper on Religious Freedom: Freedom of Religion Guaranteed, Religious Rights Well Protected* was published ten days before former President Jiang Zemin's visit to the United States. This paper consisted of five sections:
- The situation of religions in China, statistics and information.
- Religious liberty is protected by law.
- Legal administration and supervision of religious liberty.
- The Chinese government supports independence and autonomy in the management of religious affairs.
- The government protects the right of freedom of religious belief for ethnic minorities.

Clarification of the Constitutional Clause on Religion

On the surface, the Constitution and other government documents claim to protect religious freedom. But do they do so in reality? In 1997 at a conference held at the University of Hong Kong, Liu Peng of the Chinese Academy of Social Sciences clarified China's definition of religious freedom. For our better understanding, the important part of his speech is broken down by points and quoted as follows (*Tripod*, XIX (113), p. 17):

- Religion is accepted by the state on the supposition that it recognizes the state's political authority, accepts its leadership in all social spheres, and carries out its politics.
- The state administration manages religious organizations that are not involved in government administration, the judiciary, or education.
- The role of religion in society is strictly limited... Every patriotic organization must accept the leadership of the Communist Party and the government.

The Central government reiterated this statement in Document No. 6, 1991.
- These official pronouncements indicate clearly that the relationship between the Chinese Communist Party, State, and religious organizations is that of leading and being led...
- These religious groups are managed by the government and must carry out Party and government policies.
- While the religious groups are independent in terms of administrative and organizational relationships, they are no different politically from those institutions under the direct leadership of the government...
- This means that religions in China are proscribed from involvement in administration, judicial affairs, and all forms of education, whether in schools, in correspondence courses, or in the media...
- According to the analysis above, church and state relations in China fit under *state dominance over religion...*
- Obviously, this policy of the freedom of religious belief is based not on any awareness of theism or a concept of religious values, but rather on the realistic and pragmatic consideration that religion can serve the political goal of the Party and State.

In addition to the above clarification of China's position on religious freedom, we can further elaborate on Article 36 of the *Constitution* by the following comments (in italic) following each official statement:

- "Citizens of the People's Republic of China enjoy freedom of religious belief" *only when the belief is accepted by the government.*

In 1999 the People's Congress introduced and passed the legislation against religious cults, targeted especially the Falun Gong sect. Members of Falun Gong have since been persecuted in China. Furthermore, according to World Journal (5) five founders of the South China Church, a Protestant sect, were sentenced to death for breaking the new Cult Law and for committing violent offenses with intent. One of them, Li Ying, was a woman. Another ten members of the same church were given various sentences from two years to an indefinite length of time. Again on January 9, 2002 World Journal (p. A1) reported the arrest in Xiamen of a Hong Kong merchant, Lai Kwang Keung, smuggling 30,000 copies of the New Testament from Hong Kong to an evangelical underground church. If Lai is found guilty, he would be given death sentence. Following the arrest of Lai, the External Department of the government of China issued a statement that no other country should interfere with the judicial independence of China.

- No state organ, public organization or individual may compel citizens to believe in, or not to believe in, any religion; nor may they discriminate against citizens who believe in, or do not believe in, any religion. *Those who publicly profess their religions may not apply for government jobs. This is discrimination.*
- The state protects normal religious activities. *Here normal means only the activities of those churches registered with and under government supervision.*
- Religious bodies and religious affairs are not subject to any foreign domination. *Only the official "Three-Self" churches are legal entities for government*

protection. Other churches such as the underground communities are subject to persecution.

It can be seen therefore that Article 36 of the Constitution concerning religious freedom is not inclusive but discriminatory in nature. There is no legislation in the criminal code to protect believers (6). Based on the previous discourse, can we not conclude that there is no real religious policy in China? China has instead a government policy of control over religion.

Methods of Religious Control

In China, government oversees religion by a chain of national, provincial and local regulations. The process starts from the top with the Religious Affairs Bureau and the Public Security Bureau, down to the Trade Unions, the youth groups, the Women's Association, Neighborhood committees or even the Street Offices (7).

Throughout my study tour, I learned that there was no uniform implementation of religious policies. Each policy has two versions: one for the information of the general public and one for party members for implementation. Furthermore, implementation varies according to geographic location. When certain religious activities were considered beneficial to the local community, security personnel were instructed to turn a blind eye to them. Examples include a clinic, a home for the aged, and kindergartens set up by underground church members in a remote town within the boundary of my study.

Wang Zuoan, deputy director-general of the State Administration for Religious Affairs under the State Council, openly acknowledged the difficulty of a fair implementation of the national religious policy, especially when such policy is to be implemented by provincial governments which choose their own religious officials. He remarked,

Anything can happen in a big country like China. Very often, the central Government's policies are good but they become twisted at the local level (8).

Furthermore, Wang Zuoan also stressed that the purpose of a national religious policy is to protect the believers as well. According to Wang, the central administration's duty is to execute rulings on religious matters by the Communist Party and the State Council and to make sure that government agencies follow the law in administering religious organizations which are considered by the government as "social groups". He further elaborated on this aspect of "protecting the believers" as below:

> We emphasize 'rule by law' now. I often tell provincial religious officials why we draft all these rules is because we need to restrict government behaviour. What it means is when government rules, it must rule in accordance with the regulations. [Local cadres] can't supersede the rules. And you [local cadres] can't introduce a rule because this will help you to suppress the public. You can't say that when we have a religious regulation, then we have something special to deal with religions. No, you can't just do what you want, you must follow the rules." (9)

Government control of seminaries in the Open Church includes the supervision of political indoctrination in the curriculum, and the administration of a political examination based on Document 6 to final year students before their ordination. (10). Some seminaries and convents also submit monthly reports to the Religious Affairs Bureau on donations received, visits by people from Hong Kong and abroad and other happenings.

In addition, the government uses the Chinese Catholic Patriotic Association (CCPA) and the Three-Self Patriotic Christian Association as non-governmental agencies to coordinate a number of things. This includes the implementation and publicity of its policy, liaison with the outside Catholic and Protestant churches, and accepting outside financial donations for various projects such as church repairs, clinics, day care and wells. In short, as a non-governmental organization (NGO) the CCPA gives a better image of freedom of religion in China to outsiders. However, CCPA in reality is not an NGO. The government has put its own employees as some of the directors.

In the final analysis, all religions are caught in an entanglement of regulations within the boundaries of control, and this is particularly true of Catholicism because of its ecclesial -hierarchical structure and its relations to the Vatican. Next to the Falun Gong, Catholicism is most feared by the Chinese government for its structural organization as a potential subversion of the communist regime, as seen against the historical backdrops in Eastern Europe during the eighties.

Orthodoxy of Christian Teaching in China

It is a consolation to note, however, that in as far as the government control is concerned the doctrine and theology of Christianity has not changed in China. Bishop Fu Tieshan, president of the CCPA, made the following statement to defend the autonomy of the Catholic Church in China:

> In terms of the autonomous church with its own administration, we are here talking about the political aspects, of economy, and ecclesiastical and administrative affairs, and not of dogma to be believed, or of the precepts of the Church to be practiced. The Chinese church in terms of faith is equal to all the other churches in the world, belongs to the same faith,

administers the same baptism, and faithful to the one, holy, Catholic and apostolic Church. The bishops, the priests and the faithful in China are the same as the bishops, priests and faithful in the rest of the world and they pray daily for the Holy Father. (11).

Similarly, in his overseas visits Bishop Ting Quon-Fen, President of the Chinese Patriotic Christian Church, has affirmed the orthodoxy of Christian teaching in the Protestant Church. Using the Bible as the basic tool the various Christian denominations have harmonized their main theological positions to form one Christian (Protestant) Church.

Is There Real Religious Freedom in China

As we conclude this chapter, we can answer our earlier questions as follows:

- China today does not really have religious freedom according to Western standard. Within the context of the Chinese leadership, there is religious freedom because they define what freedom should include. In general, law protects such freedom as it exists within the prescribed confines.
- There is no real religious policy in China. Instead, China has a government policy of control over religion.
- Only those religions recognized by the Chinese authority, and are registered with the government, receive legal protection. All other forms of religion, such as the Underground or House Church and others considered as cults (for example, Falun Gong) are constantly undergoing government persecution.

Future Trend in the Development of Religion in China

Today, Chinese communism exists only in name. It has become totalitarianism under Deng's open-door policy. If the leaders are true communists, they should have no fear of religion. According to Marxism, religion will go away on its own with development in education and science. As many people in China today have lost their faith in the communist party and its leadership for an open and just society, there is also a corresponding loss of their moral spirit and strength to sustain and nourish their daily life. Crimes are becoming rampant in Chinese society because greed has taken over the human spirit. In fact, many people in China today believe that money is their only "god".

The Chinese Socialist Market Economy is a euphemism for capitalism under this dictatorship. As there is no sign of political reform while the economic system has been rapidly undergoing transformation for over twenty years, there is a subtle call for political restructuring from both within and outside the leadership circle. Former President Jiang Zemin was reported by *World Journal* (12) that he had earlier suggested that capitalists be considered for membership in the Communist Party to harmonize the discrepancy between economic and political reform. According to another issue of the paper (13), the next question for the leadership debate at the 16th CCP Congress of delegates in 2002 would be communist membership for religious leaders. The paper posed this question, "Why not?" The leadership has gradually come to realize that religion has a stabilizing influence on society. Seeing the prevailing social vice, President Jiang has recently been advocating Chinese traditional virtues and values as the means for ruling the country.

In fact, the deputy of the Political Reform Office in the State Secretariat, Pan Yue, was quoted by *World Journal* (14) as saying the following. The communist concept of "religion is the opiate of the people" has already cost China a high price in view of the present social disorder. In his article *Marxist idea of religion must keep pace with time,* he points out that "the present lapse of religious faith in China is a potential harm to society, because religion teaches people to practice virtues which are sustained by religious faith. A country without sustaining faith will not be able to have a footing in the world community of nations." Since he was a high profile person in the government, there was speculation that the Chinese leadership was considering a new balance between religious freedom and government control. The recent establishment of Department of Christianity Studies at some leading universities in China, such as Beijing University, is an indication that religion, particularly Christianity, is receiving positive attention from the Chinese leadership.

In fact, former President Jiang, at the recent Religious Affairs Conference, stated his position that religion will continue to assert its influence on social development and stability, and that the leadership must pave the way for a better harmonization of socialism and religion. But he continued to point out that religions in China must be self-sustained, self-administered and self-propagating without any foreign domination (15). It was clear that Jiang Zemin was reiterating the importance of religious autonomy from foreign control, while stressing the important role of religion in Chinese society. It appears that the future of both the Catholic Church and the Protestant Church in China must follow this official direction if they are to grow and to meet the underlying objective of bringing the Christian message closer to the masses.

Chapter VII

THE CURRENT RELIGIOUS POLICY OF CHINA RELATING TO CHRISTIANITY

End Notes

1. Information used for this chapter comes from my interview data and various journals as indicated throughout the text. Two words can summarize the religious policy of China: religious control.
2. Mi, Michael C. Five Obstacles to Sino-Vatican Reconciliation. Tripod, XVI (95), p.5-21.
3. Bush, Richard C. Jr. Religion in Communist China. Nashville, TN: Abingdon Press,1970, pp. 105-107
4. Information for this section comes from my observation and interview in China, various newspapers and journals, and from Patricia Leung's book, *Sino-Vatican Relations*, pp. 116-133. Her book is very helpful for the understanding of religious development in China since 1978.
5. *World Journal*, (2001, Dec. 31), p. A1. (Chinese Daily newspaper published in Hong Kong, with various overseas versions such as Vancouver Version).
6. All religious groups, including those of Buddhism and Taoism, are hoping for legislation of religious rights.
7. Religious control is carried very systematically in China, from the top level branching out to the local level. The same technique was used during the Cultural Revolution when everyone was spying on everyone, including members within the same family. Some stories I gathered were horrible. The son gave information about the father to the Street Office, which in turn passed it on to a higher level. The father was eventually accused of "ideological crime" and publicly tried in the street by mobs.
8. Daniel Kwan (2002, March 29). Regulator of religious activity stresses 'rule by law'. *South China Morning Post*, p. 7.
9. *Ibid.*

10. Every young priest ordained after 1985 has received political indoctrination in the seminary which is partially funded by the government. This is another example of religious control. The Underground Church, being clandestine, has not undergone this political process.
11. *Asia News, and Mondo et Missione Supplement*, No. 10, 1997, pp. 51-58, also *Tripod* (XIX (113), p. 21)
12. *World Journal* (2001, December 14) p. 10A. (Chinese daily newspaper published in Hong Kong, having overseas editions).
13. 2001, Dec. 24, p. A10)
14. 2001, Dec. 23, p. 10.
15. *Sing Tao Daily*, Dec. 13, 2001, p. A13.

CHAPTER XI

WILL CHRISTIANITY EVER TAKE ROOT IN CHINA? A PERSONAL PERSPECTIVE

After reading the previous chapters we now have come to a better idea of the Church situation in China in relation to the state religious policy. We can now speculate what the future holds for Christianity to take root in Chinese soil.

When we say that Western culture has its roots in Judeo-Christian heritage, we do not refer to the number of people attending church every Sunday. We do not refer to religious piety. Instead, we talk about how Christianity has helped develop personal and societal values such as mutual care, equality, brotherly love, and the value and the dignity of the human person, among many other traits. Most important of all is the rights of the individual.

As an example, in Western Europe in particular, not too many people attend a church service on Sundays. This is particularly true in Belgium or Holland. The churches are less than half-filled. Yet, the society is a caring one in terms of looking after the aged and the young, or the sick and the underprivileged. The dignity of the person is respected.

If we look at China in 2008 when the country declared to the world that it has advanced economically to become a power by hosting the Olympic Games and the successful launching of its third manned space mission, we do not get the real picture. Yes, indeed, the material quality of life has improved for about one-third of the population, but how does society as a whole react to the other two-thirds that are still marginalized without the secured provision of the most basics of life such as food, education, health care, old-age securities, and others? Most important of all, in the competition for a better life, society as a whole has lost the traditional values as taught by the ancient sages such as Confucius for a caring social order. A recent media survey revealed that people in China spend the least for charity. The 500 or so billionaires have not come out to contribute significantly to the improvement of those who suffered in the earthquakes or other disasters. Furthermore, the recent tainted milk product scandals (see Appendix) have shown the greed at every level of society. Cheating and taking advantage of each other in order to become rich has become the rule of the day. The situation is getting pathetic when the government would not allow victims to ask for redress or compensation for fear of upsetting the economic order. The ideal of compassion is gone. Clearly there is a moral void.

In our earlier discussions we have seen that Christianity is filling up this void in China. But we need the institution of the church to spread the good message of Christian love which is lacking in the Confucius moral teaching. We have seen that even government officials in China have acknowledged the positive role of Christianity in the transformation of the Chinese society. As a result, a number of universities have set up departments of Christian Studies and organized exchange programs with universities in Europe, North America and Australia. Indeed, the Communist government of China welcomes Christianity if it is developed along the principle of the Three Self Movements without outside interference in the administration such as foreign missionary groups or societies. Many outside Christian groups may have the good intention to help the Church in China, but often they challenge the Chinese religious policy and cause the government to take a more rigid religious control.

No matter what the future holds, there is one question we must ask: why do people in China go to Church? My informal interviews with people in China after Sunday Service reveal several major reasons: fellowship, psychological peace, hope (petition for divine intervention), and the search for meaning in life. Statements such as the following are very inspiring (1):

- Every time when I am inside the church, I feel an unspoken peace within me. I offer all my troubles to God, and I trust Jesus will tell me what to do about my life.
- I like to meet my relatives or friends after church. We chat and we go to have breakfast or lunch together.
- I make new friends in church, and I trust my church friends more than other friends.
- My mother is terminally sick, and the doctor said her case is hopeless. It is only by coming to attend Mass that I feel comforted and strengthened.
- We have too many social problems. I feel despair and fearful of what is going to happen to me. My husband is doing good business, but has become involved with another woman. I come to pray for help.

These statements have confirmed the view that in a socialist or any society there is a need for religious faith. Therefore, Zhao Fusan, former deputy director of the Chinese Academy of Social Sciences and a scholar in Christianity, asks the following searching questions (2):

- Is it not possible that the understanding of social contradictions has been deepened because of religion's critical attitude towards them?
- Is it not possible that others have learned from religions an attitude of selflessness, which leads them to work for the social liberation of others?
- If religion is only the "opium of the people" how can we explain that the satisfaction of religious needs has motivated people to be more supportive of socialist reform?
- How can we explain that non-believers are sometimes not as socially advanced as believers are?

Zhao concludes that in consideration of the positive contributions of religions to society today, their negative influences in socialist China are comparatively unimportant. Here lies the challenge to the Chinese Communist Party: accept the fact that Christianity, rooted in the Chinese culture, is making a positive contribution in the reconstruction of China.

Christianity as Institutionalized Religion

When we discuss Christianity as a religion rather than a philosophy, we can only do so in the context of its institutionalization as the Christian Church. By its historical development, this Christian Church has split into three major denominations, namely the Roman Catholic Church, the Eastern Orthodox Church and the Protestant Church. Only the Roman Catholic Church and the Protestant Church have so far made significant inroads in China. Hence, when we discuss the future of Christianity in China, we can only do so in its institutionalized framework, namely the future of the Catholic Church and the Protestant Church.

In the previous chapters I have explained the history and the contemporary political, economic and social conditions in China leading to a firmly committed religious policy of the People's Republic of China. Such policy requires that all religions must adapt to the political philosophy of the government. Translated in concrete terms, the policy means that all religious institutions must register with the government, which will in turn direct and supervise their activities and manifestations. Furthermore, all religious institutions must be free from foreign dominance and interference, and as such all churches must become self-administering, self-supporting and self-propagating. In the case of the Protestant Church, it has developed into a fully independent national Chinese Christian Church having the Bible as its basic doctrinal foundation, and has received due recognition and even support from the central government. In the case of the Chinese Catholic Church, it has become a national church that has severed its political, economic and administrative link with the Vatican, but still keeps the Pope as the spiritual head. In terms of orthodoxy, everything is the same as the universal Catholic Church.

The Future of the Catholic Church in China

In the eyes of some members of the universal Church, the problem of the Chinese Catholic Church lies in communion with the Pope, because the Pope no longer appoints bishops in China. As the Vicar of Christ, the current Pope, Benedict XVI, maintains that he must have the absolute and universal authority over this important issue. It is the appointment of bishops, rather than the moving of the Vatican Embassy from Taipei to Beijing, that has become the Gordian knot in the normalization of Sino-Vatican relations. However, it is crucial to understand whether or not the bishop is recognized by the Pope in the ecclesial process is comparatively less important than his ability to lead his diocese to usher in the Kingdom of God, for God is bigger than the Church (3).

The Catholic Church was once very proud of itself as a universal church. This means "uniformity" all over the world: the same language (Latin) for the celebration of the Mass, the same liturgy, the same requirement for the ordination of priests, and the same Canon law. But this universality is hurting more than helping many dioceses in our present pluralistic and multicultural world (4). For example, some years ago, the Bishop of the Canadian North kept asking the Vatican for permission to bend the rule of compulsory celibacy in order to ordain suitable married aboriginal candidates. In the aboriginal culture, a celibate person is not a desirable person for any leadership position, and hence the bishop hardly received response to his priestly vocational appeal. Today, with an area more than half of Canada in size, there are only four aging priests to serve the diocese. Is this what Christ intends to happen?

Should the unity of the "universal Church" be upheld at all cost at the expense of the people, in this age of liberalism, pluralism and multiculturalism? Should not each national church determine its own response to the needs?

Within the universal Church, there have been many discussions about the local election of bishops, more involvement of the laity in the decision-making process, and more authority for the regional and local church. By having a free election of the bishops, the Chinese Church has taken a step ahead of the Vatican in this governance reform, and before they go any further following the example of the English Reformation in 1534, Rome should take measures to avoid any attempt of schism by anyone. In the meantime, a compromise could be reached whereby the election, appointment and the consecration of bishops in China could be done collegially by both Rome and the Chinese Catholic Church to attain the goal of universal communion (5).

Clearly there is a difference of perspectives between Beijing and the Vatican. Beijing has repeatedly indicated that it is ready to normalize relation with Rome but the Vatican "needs to show good faith". In an interview in March 2002 by *South China Morning Post*, Wang Zuoan, deputy director-general of the State Administration for Religious Affairs under the State Council, said that "although Beijing had noted steps taken by the Catholic Church to mend ties with China, the Holy See needed to do more to prove its sincerity." He was repeating Beijing's two basic demands: the Vatican must sever ties with Taipei and must not interfere in China's internal affairs. By "Vatican's interference", he was referring to the papal appointment of bishops and the canonization issue two years ago. He pointed out that the canonization event was "not merely coincidental" because it took place on October 1, 2000, being 51st anniversary of the establishment of the People's Republic of China. Therefore he said that the Pope "owes us an apology. We have read his statement, but we don't see any apology in it."

In response to the Pope's statement that both China and Rome "should not get tangled in history and look forward to the future," the deputy director-general remarked that Beijing did not want to "get tangled" in history. However, he also emphasized that China could not afford turning a blind eye to the historical past. He added that when the Vatican named various foreign and Chinese martyrs as saints, Rome was reasserting its own view of history, and was asking Chinese Catholics to emulate these "saints", contrary to what China holds as the historical truth. He further denounced the Vatican's collaboration with the Underground Church by secretly ordaining underground Catholic bishops, thus nurturing its own forces in Chinese territory, and causing a split in the Catholic Church in China (6).

With Beijing being so adamant in upholding its religious policy, and with Rome being so authoritative in defending its power to appoint bishops, an impasse in the Sino-Vatican relations has been created with no sign of change. This deadlock is further strengthened by the following events:

- The undivided loyalty to the Pope by the Underground clergy in China;
- The unwillingness of the Vatican to adapt itself to the situation in China;
- The division of the Catholic Church in China – the development of the Open and Underground churches;
- The inability of the Vatican to come up with a policy to handle the present ecclesial confusion in China.

So, where do we go from here?

We must consider the development of the CCC in the context of a rapidly changing Chinese society with a new and fast growing intellectual climate. As China is now a member of the World Trade Organization, its political and economic structure is also rapidly changing. The ultimate problem for the Church is not its survival, but meaningful and realistic evangelization. Both the Underground Church and the Open Church must understand this challenge. All concerned must be able to read the signs of the times and start helping to heal the division within the CCC so that both Churches may become reconciled for a common purpose — a meaningful evangelization of God's Kingdom to take root in Chinese soil.

Allow me to invite Bishop Aloysius Jin Luxian of Shanghai to share with us his vision of the Catholic Church in China today. Bishop Jin is acknowledged as a visionary leader of the CCC both inside and outside China. He is theologically articulate and knowledgeable of Vatican II and the universal Church. At an open forum at Louven University in Belgium, he gave the following observations in his address (7):

- In recalling the four centuries of Catholic history in China, we must conclude that, with notable exceptions such as Ricci and others of rare foresight, those in authority pursued a policy of total uniformity in all church matters. Neither our culture, nor our traditional sages were accorded the respect and evaluation that was their due.
- The people of China have chosen socialism... We must take part in the life and destiny of our country, and experience its joys and sorrows. It has wiped out starvation. The national dignity has been restored... The Chinese Church, administered by Chinese Catholics is patriotic and law-abiding, and it maintains its independence and autonomy. It has adapted itself to the actual situation of China. Perhaps the truth of what Cardinal Lekai, primate of Hungary, said applies here: "I would never attempt to go back, but rather to push history forward."
- In the past the Church has insisted on uniformity. Complete and absolute control was exercised over everything. Too much control stifles vitality. The core of Roman civilization was "power: which is to say authority and law. "Charity," the most important commandment of Our Savior, was neglected. We clearly perceive that it is easier to abandon a dead language [Latin] than to give up attachment to power.
- Pluralism means to try with all our effort to preach the Gospel in the midst of all kinds of social systems. Already more than one billion people live under the socialist system. Ought not the attitude of Catholics throughout the whole world be this: to understand and support the pioneering efforts of Catholics who live under this system, to draw conclusions from their experiences, successes as well as failures, and

to encourage them. For their witness is all the more valuable as their situation is totally different. The dream of interference and domination by relying on the financial and military forces of the great powers has been disastrous in the past, and it will be even more so in the future. The reason is apparent: because it does not conform to the spirit of Jesus Christ.
- Permit me to cite here the words of the famous Christian theologian Oscar Cullman: "Where the Holy Spirit is at work, he gives birth to diversity. However, each action does not result in fragmentation. Each member of the body carries out his/her mission, which is directed towards unity."
- In conclusion, I wish to repeat the words of Isaiah: "My ways are not your ways." When many Catholics in Europe thought that the church in China was dead, the Lord prepared a new way for us. For the first time in history the Catholic Church of China is conscious of being a truly local Chinese and independent Catholic Church. This is the content of my message.

With the old mentality of church hierarchy that the Pope must be in control of the appointment of bishops, as shown in the papal pastoral letter in 2007 to the Church in China, conservative leaders in the Vatican failed to see that spreading the gospel is more important than adhering to a church structure. Such structure is considered by many to be rigid and outdated by today's standard. The appointment of bishops by the Pope is comparatively a recent procedure of the Catholic Church. Authors such Peter Huizing and Knut Walf, Leonard Swidler and Arlene Widler, and Giuseppe Alberigo and Anton Weiler have pointed out that historically before 1900, the monarch in each country appointed their bishops (8).

Dan Overmyer, Professor Emeritus of the Department of Asian Studies at the University of British Columbia, has this to say about institutions that never want to change:

> Social institutions that may have been appropriate at one time may become instruments of control and oppression, if carried on unchanged...We need to maintain some form of stable social structure without letting it become rigid and oppressive. Some religious traditions attempt to stop time and change with the claim that they are based on a self-defined, absolute and unchanging dimension of reality. (9).

For the sake of spreading the Gospel in China, perhaps Rome should re-evaluate with vision and insight its position in the current impasse of Sino-Vatican relations. Perhaps the next Pope and the next leaders of China would come to a compromise for a new relationship. By then Rome might have lost the fertile ground in China for Christian evangelization. Rome lost such an opportunity over the Rites issue three hundred years ago. Will it make the same mistake again? Let's hope history does not repeat itself.

John Henry Newman (1801-1890), an Anglican theologian who turned Catholic in 1845 and was made a cardinal in 1879, is often quoted as saying "To live here below is to change, and to have changed often is to reach perfection". If the Vatican is unwilling to change to accommodate the needs of the people in China, and as God is bigger than the Church, the only option for the Chinese Catholic Church is to form its own rite as a separate but legitimate Christian entity, in order to meaningfully proclaim the Kingdom of God on Chinese soil.

It appears that Protestant Christianity is working along this direction. In spite of harsh persecution during the Cultural Revolution, its membership has greatly increased

— more than that of the CCC (10) in the ratio of 1 to 3. This is possible because the Chinese Protestant Church has adapted itself to Chinese feelings and aspirations. It has transformed its teaching to accommodate the government's high ideals of a socialist Chinese society.

Earlier we mentioned the well-known American historian John Fairbanks who uses his theory of "Impact and Response" to explain historical development in China since the Opium War. In the past, China had to respond to the impact of the west; any response in the wrong direction had brought chaos in China. Today, China is making its impact on the West, including the Vatican. In economic terms, the market is there for the Church of Rome. It all depends on the priority of the Vatican.

Does Rome want to bring Christ to the vast Chinese populace, or to re-establish its authority and maintain its control through a rigid ecclesiastical structure in a country, which has long had a strong spirituality at the root of its culture, even before the birth of Christ? Rome has made its mistakes in the past; will it make the same mistake again and lose this golden opportunity to evangelize? With the current relaxation of economic and social policies in China, we can only pray that "a continuing clash between these two centers of authority which have conflicting concepts of what constitutes that true source of authority, may change into reconciliation" soon (11).

The Future of the Protestant Church

In contrast to the Chinese Catholic Church, we have already discussed that the Protestant Church is free from this authority issue currently afflicting the Catholic Church in China, and is expanding fast. In his book, *China's Catholics*, Richard Madsen (12) makes the following observation of the Protestant Church in China:

Although conversions are taking place in the cities, where most Protestants lived before 1949, the hottest part of the Protestant fever seems to be in the countryside. Conversions take place through itinerant lay preachers, most preaching an evangelical Protestant doctrine...Often they convert whole villages, which organize themselves through lay leaders around a life of Bible study and worship after the itinerant evangelists move on. Although the faith brings no material benefits – it appears to bring great spiritual consolation to people fearful of the materialism, competitiveness, and corruption of the new society. . . . Their faith perhaps gives them a promise of healing and salvation as they enter the uncharted seas of a new market economy.

The current religious policy of China has successfully combined all Protestant denominations into one vibrant Chinese Christian Church. The Protestant Church has followed the principle of "Three Self Movement" to harmonize with the current Chinese political and cultural climate. Protestant Christians in China do not see martyrdom in the present age and time as a way to salvation. A progressive Catholic thinker from Gonzaga University has pointed out to me the startling fact that the underground church members in China are not suffering for their faith, but for a structural system: the Canon Law and the hierarchical structure of the Church of Rome (13).

As early as the 1950s, Ronald Owen Hall, Anglican Bishop of Hong Kong, took the Chinese religious policy in a positive way. He insisted that the church in China must adapt to the national reconciliation. He firmly believed that the communist government was dedicated to the welfare of the people and therefore could be considered a "minister of God" to overthrow evil. In his view, the church must accept the government not because of its political ideology but because of the reality that it is the governing body. The church therefore had to understand the government (14).

The Protestant church in China has been growing much faster than its Catholic counterpart, and can be considered as the "emergent church". One factor stands out to explain the disparity. The Protestant church concentrates on the spreading the Gospel and harmonizes well with the religious policy of the government. Furthermore, according to Richard Madsen (15) "conversion in the Protestant Church is search for the new rather than a clinging to the old, a search made possible by the new market economy...Conversion appears to bring great spiritual consolation to people fearful of the materialism, competitiveness, and corruption of the new society. The Protestants preach a conservative morality, emphasizing the importance of family and community, but their faith perhaps gives them a promise of healing and salvation as they enter the uncharted seas of a new market economy. One is tempted to speculate that while the Catholicism is a way for rural people to shelter themselves from modernity, Protestantism is a way to strength and fortify them as they undertake a dangerous pilgrimage into modernity."

Protestantism and Catholicism Contrasted

The Catholic Church in China, on the other hand, is constantly struggling with the government over the matter of legitimate church hierarchy in relationship to the Vatican. At the end of the day, the struggle does not leave much energy for the clergy to spread the message of the Gospel, particularly among the intellectuals, nor for offering pastoral care for the faithful. Today within China, there are more educated individuals or intellectuals participating in the Protestant post-denominational church than in the Catholic Church. The information I gathered in China indicates that more and more "cultural Christians" (that is, intellectuals who consider themselves Christians as they submerge themselves in the study of Christianity without going through baptism to avoid any political entanglement) are siding with the Protestant church.

The best example to illustrate the contrast between the progress made by Protestant and Catholic evangelization can be found in the modern city of Shanghai which has boosted its population from over a million in 1978 to over 17 million in 2008. Before the liberation in 1949 the Protestants numbered 30,000. Today, their numbers have exceeded 700,000, with 50 million Bibles having been printed by the Amity Press in Nanjing for the membership. On the contrary, the number of Catholics before the liberation was 100,000 (more then 3 times of the protestants), but in 2008, their number was only 150,000 (about 22 percent of the Protestant population). This is definitely a decline from the pre-liberation level. And the number of the Bibles printed for use is comparatively insignificant. Bishop Aloysius Jin made the following observation:

> Each of us Catholics should take the spreading of the Gospel seriously, coordinating with the priests and Sisters in the work of evangelization. We priests, Sisters and seminarians, who lived a consecrated life, cannot just finish the Holy Sacrifice of the Mass and the reading of the breviary, then close the gate of the church, and spend the bulk of our time on the Internet or watching TV...The gate of the church should be open during daytime; the priests and Sisters should always warmly welcome visitors... [for them] to go further and find out more about the Jesus Christ whom we proclaim...(16)

Furthermore, with the current one-child population policy in China, parents are reluctant to encourage their only son to become a celibate priest for the Church. Consequently, as in other parts of the world the Catholic Church in China has already experienced a shortage of qualified candidates for the priesthood. With a foreseeable shortage of priests of strong leadership the future of the Catholic Church in China is less than certain. The root of the problem is clear: the Catholic Church emphasizes its historical legitimacy rather than the spread of the gospel message, while its Protestant counterpart focuses on the Gospel message rather than its organizational structure.

Political Harmonization

Last but not least, political harmonization is now a part of the Chinese culture and is important for the future survival of the Church. American historian John D.Young, who specializes in cultural harmonization in the study of Matteo Ricci and Confucianism, sums up the church-state relationship in China as follows:

> As long as the Chinese Communist Party is in charge, those who are involved with spreading the Christian message (or even other religious beliefs) have no choice but to co-operate whenever necessary. (17)

This is particularly true with the Protestant church whose adherents are now numbered almost 21 million by official statistics in December 2007. On the other hand, the number of Catholics are just a little over 5 million, about 25% of the Protestants. (18) This can be understood when so much energy is sapped in the church by the dispute between Beijing and Rome over where the authority lies in the appointment of bishops, and the church relies on clericalism for the preaching of dogma and administration of the church. On the contrary, the Protestants rely heavily on lay involvement in the preaching of the Gospel using the Bible as their basic tool, and have a close and harmonious relationship with both the Central Government and other fellow churches and societies overseas. They have exerted an influence on family, neighbors and society. Hence, according to Professor Richard Madsen, the contribution of the Catholic Church to social transformation has not been as significant as the Protestant Church. (19)

Conclusion: The Church with a Vision

Therefore, for the Church to succeed in the future, it must have a vision of its mission. It must be able to inculturate in the Chinese soil and put less emphasis on ecclesial legalism, and more stress on the teaching of Christ in social justice and mutual concern. Like Jesus, the Church must go beyond the limits of the church law to serve the unfortunate, the hungry, the weak, the vulnerable and the needy. In short, it must be able to help people in their search for a meaningful life in a changing Chinese society that is becoming more and more greedy and self-centered.

World Vision Canada vice-president Don Posterski in his book *The Future Faith Church* (20) has this to say:

> Thou shalt not be paranoid…We're so separated and isolated, we've lost a view of our potential…it will be the local church, not the national denominations, that will lead the way…The church is more than experiencing God. It is caring for the local and global labour.

He goes on to say that we must be faithful to the faith and relevant to the culture so that we will succeed to bring the message of the Gospel to other people. He adds further that the most important action is to show by our examples the love of God and the love of our neighbors (21). Similarly, Martin Luther King also says hat "It has been my conviction that any religion that professes to be concerned about the souls of men and is not concerned about the social and economic conditions that scar the soul, is a spiritually moribund religion only waiting for the day to be buried." Accordingly, a number of clergy both from Hong Kong and abroad have been staying in China, not to preach the gospel as required by the law, but to bear witness to Christ by teaching English, philosophy and other disciplines.

In a similar manner, a number of overseas Chinese Protestants have organized themselves to reach out to the remote provinces of Ningxia and Gansu in China. Among others, they include a group of Canadian doctors and engineers of Chinese descent under the name of "World Vision China" to visit remote areas to donate their medical and engineering services. In their recent document, *"Water Projects, Medical Support, Love Spreading, Hope Sharing"* they reported they have witnessed active faith among the local Christians. Furthermore, Protestant churches in North America also actively encourage members to join short-term evangelization programs. A great number of early retirees support this program either by financial contribution or by becoming evolved in the effort of evangelism under the disguise of teaching job skills to the people in the remote areas. Even some Buddhist sects have joined the evangelization bandwagon. For example, the Tsu-Chi Buddhists in Taiwan have now established an off-shoot in mainland China to do charity work similar to that of the International Caritas, and have received recognition from the mainland government.

We can better understand the future of Christianity in China by the number of Bibles centrally printed in Nanjing by the Amity Press in cooperation with the International Bible Society. By the end of 2006, this government-approved publishing house had printed a total of 53,219,332 Bibles for use within China. Of these, 38,690,000 copies were published for the Protestant churches in China, while

590,000 copies were distributed to the Catholic churches. (22) It is interesting to see that the Chinese Amity Press has even printed 6,600,000 copies of the Bible for overseas Chinese churches. This is truly a grace that is so amazing!

Walbert Buhlmann (23) in his book, *The Search for God: an Encounter with the Peoples and Religions of Asia*, has prophesized that the centre of gravity for Christianity will be in the Pacific Rim, away from Europe. In spite of the severe persecution of Christians during the Cultural Revolution from 1965 to 1977, the Christian population has more than quadrupled in China. The Holy Spirit has been quietly working in the Chinese Church. Although the number is small compared to the vast population of 1.35 billion in China today, we must not forget the Gospel parable: the mustard seed is tiny, but it grows and multiplies fast, under the guidance of the Holy Spirit.

CHAPTER XI

WILL CHRISTIANITY EVER TAKE ROOT IN CHINA? A PERSONAL PERSPECTIVE

End Notes

1. During my study tour in China in the past eight years, I have occasions to say hello to parishioners after Sunday service. It is part of the Chinese culture to greet each other after liturgical celebrations. To break the ice, you usually say the following: good morning, or you got up early today, or have you had your breakfast (or lunch) yet, etc. And so I was able to start asking some questions concerning their faith, by introducing myself as a Christian from Canada.
2. Zhao Fusan, "A Reconsideration of Religion", in *Zhongguo Shehui Kexue*, no. 3, 1986. Translated by Fen Shize in *Social Sciences in China*. Beijing, Autumn 1986, quoted in Pro Mundi Vita, no.115, June 1990, p.12.
3. Theologian Fr. Kenan Osborne expressed this view in his presentation of Anthony Jordan Lecture Series in March, 2001 at Newman Theological College in Edmonton, Canada., reported by Western Catholic Reporter on April 9, 2001 under the heading "God bigger than the Church". What he says applies to the Church in China. The Kingdom of God comes first before considering any legal legitimacy of the appointment of bishops.
4. "The challenge for the Church is to follow the new culture and try to evangelize it...the adult life cycle is now characterized by unpredictability," Paul Andre Giguere said at the Institute de Pastorale de Montreal. For a full text, consult Western Catholic Reporter (2001 Oct. 01), p. 4
5. China might want to consider the Vietnamese model of the appointment of bishops. In this model, the Vietnamese government suggests three names to the Pope for appointment. If this has authority issue with Beijing, another alternative is for the Holy See to suggest to Beijing three candidates for each

appointment, and the Chinese government makes the final choice.
6. While in China in May 2001 I made a literature survey of the canonization issue. All media pointed out that a proclamation of Chinese saints using dubious and obscured historical records from Taiwan had certainly angered the Chinese authority. Rome had never consulted with Beijing on this issue. From the perspective of Beijing, it was definitely an assault on its sovereignty.
7. Jin is the Bishop of Shanghai and has made visits to Hong Kong, Europe and the United States. The University Parish and the China-Europe Institute sponsored this forum at Louvain University in Belgium in May 1987.
8. For a detailed discussion on this issue, consult Quinn, John R. *The Reform of the Papacy: the Costly Call to Christian Unity.* New York: Crossroad Publishing, 1999.
9. Dan Overmyer, "The World As a Holy Place", *Trek* (Summer, 2005, pp 16-17).
10. *Tsing Tao Daily,* Nov. 26, 2000, p.4; also, World Journal, (20002 March 01), p. A10.
11. Cf. Leung, Beatrice. *Sino-Vatican Relations: Problems in Conflicting Authority: 1976-1986.* Cambridge: The University Press, 1992.
12. Madsen, Richard. *China's Catholics: Tragedy and Hope in an emerging Civil Society.* Los Angeles: University of California Press, 1998, pp. 137-138.
13. Dr. Leonard Doohan is a professor theology at Gonzaga University. He pointed this out at the Scripturefest 2001 in Edmonton, Canada after his lectures on the Gospel of Mark.
14. See Deborah A. Brown. *The Anglican Church in Hong Kong and the Challenge of Transition.* Hong Kong: Centre of Asia Studies, University of Hong Kong, 1993, p.6.
15. Richard Madsen, *ibid,* pp. 237-238.
16. Aloysius Jin Luxian, "400 Years of Catholicism in Shanghais: a pastoral letter issued at Christmas 2007", in *Tripod,* Summer 2008, pp. 5-19.
17. *Tripod* XII (69), p. 57.

18. Tripod, #147, Winter 2007, p. 47, also *Sing Tao Daily* 2000, Nov. 26.
19. Richard Madsen, Ibid.
20. Posterski, Don and Gary Nelson. *Future Faith Churches: Reconnecting with the Power of the Gospel for the 21st Century.* Winfield, B.C.: Wood Lake Books, Inc.1997, pp. 2-5.
21. Ibid., p.2-9.
22. *Tripod*, #144, spring 2007, p. 30.
23. Buhlmann, Walbert. *The Search for God: an encounter with the Peoples and Religions of Asia.* New York: Orbis, 1975.

PART ONE

BIBLIOGRAPHY

Abbott, Walter (Ed.). (1966). *The Documents of Vatican II*. Trans. by Joseph Gallagher. London: Geoffrey Chapman.

Alberigo, Giuseppe and Anton Weiler (Ed.). (1972). *Election and Consensus in the Church*. New York: Herder and Herder.

Beers, Burton F. (1989). *World History: Patterns of Civilization*. Scarborough, Ontario: Prentice Hall Canada Inc., 1989.

Buhlmann, Walbert (1975). *The Search for God: an Encounter with the Peoples and Religions of Asia*. New York: Orbis.

Buhlmann, Walbert (1990). *With Eyes to See: Church and World in the Third Millenium*. New York: Maryknoll, 1990.

Bush, Richard C. Jr. (1970) *Religion in Communist China*. Nashville, TN: Abingdon Press.

Canadian Chinese Times. Edmonton, Alberta. Weekly free publication.

Canon Law Society of America (1992). *Code of Canons of the Eastern Churches. Latin- English Edition. Washington, D.C.: Canon Law Society of America, 1992.*

Catholic Life Weekly. Taipei, Taiwan.

Chan, Kim-kwong (1987). *Towards a Contextual Ecclesiology: The Catholic Church in the People's Republic of China (1979-1983): Its Life and Theological Implications.* Hong Kong: Photech Systems.

Chao, Johnathan (1998). "Is Reconciliation Possible?" *Torrent*, Nepean, Ont.: Chinese Christian Business and Professional Association.

Chiramel, Jose and K. Bharanikulangara (1993). *The Code of Canons of the Eastern Churches: A Study and Interpretation.* Alwaye, India: St. Thomas Academy for Research

Commentary on the Documents of Vatican II, Vol. I: Dogmatic Constitution on the Church; Decree on Eastern Catholic Churches (1967). New York: Herder and Herder/Palm Publishers.

The Constitution of the People's Republic of China (1982). Adopted on December 4, 1982 by The Fifth National People's Congress of the People's Republic of China at It's Fifth Session. Beijing: Foreign Languages Press.

Creswell, John W. (1994a). *Research Design: qualitative & quantitative approaches.* Thousand Oaks, CA: Sage.

Creswell, John W. (1994b). *Qualitative Inquiry and Research Design: Choosing Among Five Traditions.* Thousand Oaks, CA: Sage.

Chu, Michael, S.J. (1997). (Ed.). *The New China: A Catholic Response*. New York: Paulist Press.

Chupungco, Anscar J. (1982). *Cultural Adaptation of the Liturgy*. New York: Paulist Press.

Chupungco, Anscar J. (1992). *Liturgical Inculturation, Sacramentals, Religiosity, and Catechesis*. Collegeville, Minn.: Pueblo Book.

Coriden, James A. (1998, August 14). Punishing Dissent. *Commonweal*.

Criveller, Gianni (1997). *Preaching Christ in Late Ming China: The Jesuits' Presentation of Christ from Matteo Ricci to Giulio Aleni*. Taipei,Taiwan: Ricci Institute for Chinese Studies.

Digan, Parig. *The Christian China-Watchers: A Post-Mao Perspective*. Brussels: Pro Mundi Vita, 1978.

East Asian Pastoral Review. Manila: Philippines. (Four issues a year)

Edmonton Chinese News. Edmonton, Alberta. Weekly free publication.

Eliade, Mircea (n.d.). *A History of Religious Ideas*. Chicago: The University Press.

Ely, Margot (1991). *Doing Qualitative Research: Circles Within Circles*. London, Falmer Press.

Erlandson, D.A., Harris, E.L., Skipper, B.L. & Allen, S.D (1993). *Doing Naturalistic Inquiry: A Guide to Methods*. Newbury Park, CA: Sage.

Fang Hao (1959). *A History of Interrelations Between China and the West*, 5 vols. Taipei: Chinese Cultural Press.

Faris, John D. (1992). *The Eastern Catholic Churches: Constitution and Governance According to the Code of Canons of the Eastern Churches*. New York: Saint Maron Publications.

Fairbanks, John K. (1974). *The Cambridge History of China; vol. 10: Late Ch'ing, 1800-1911, Part 1*. Cambridge, Mass.: Harvard University Press.

Faris, John D. (1992). *Eastern Catholic Churches: Constitution and Governance*. New York: Saint Maron Publications.

Fung, Raymond (1982) (Comp. and trans.) *Households of God on China's Soil*. Geneva: World Council of Churches.

Gernet, Jacques (1985). *China and the Christian Impact: a Conflict of Cultures*. Translated by Janet Lloyd. Cambridge: The University Press.

Glesne, Corrine (1998). *Becoming Qualitative Researchers: An Introduction*. 2nd Edition. New York: Longman.

Gu Yulu (1989). *The Chinese Catholic Church: Past and Present*. Shanghai Academy of Social Sciences.

Guba, E.G., & Lincoln, Y. (1988). *Do Inquiry Paradigms Imply Inquiry Methodologies?* In D.M. Fetterman (Ed.), *Qualitative Approaches to Evaluation in Education* (pp.89-115). New York: Praeger.

Guba, E., and Lincoln, Y. (1989). *Fourth Generation Evaluation*. Newbury Park, CA: Sage.

Hay, Malcolm (1956). *Failure in the Far East: Why and How the Breach Between the Western World and China First Began*. Belgium: Wetteren.

Ho, Louis Kam-tat (1996). *Theological and Cultural Accommodation: Matteo Ricci and the Jesuit Mission in China.* Unpublished Master of Theological Studies thesis. Edmonton, Canada: St. Stephen's College, 1996.

Hong Kong Standard. A leading English Daily newspaper in Hong Kong.

Huizing, Peter and Knut Walf (Ed). (1980). *Electing Our Own bishops.* New York: The Seabury Press.

Hunter, Alan and Kim-Kwong Chan 1993). *Protestantism in Contemporary China.* Cambridge: The University Press, 1993.

Jiang Ping (1986). An Earnest Learning from the Religious Theory of Marxism and Religious Policy of the Party. Beijing: *Hongqi,* the official magazine of the CCP, issue No. 9.

Killen, Patricia O'Connell and John De Beer (1994). *The Art of Theological Reflection.* New York: Crossroad.

Kirby, Sandra and Kate McKenna (1989). *Experience, Research, Social Change: Methods from the Margins.* Toronto: Garamond Press.

Komonchak, Joseph (1998, September 12). On the Authority of Bishop's Conferences. *America,* 7-10.

Kung, Hans and Julia Ching (1998). *Christianity and Chinese Religions.* Toronto: Doubleday.

Kung Kao Po. (Hong Kong Catholic Weekly in Chinese).

Lam, Anthony S.K. (1997). *The Catholic Church in Present Day China: Through Darkness and Light.* English Edition. Hong Kong: The Holy Spirit Study Centre.

Lam, Wing-Hung (1983). *Chinese Theology in Construction.* Pasadena, CA.: William Carey Library.

Latourette, Kenneth Scott (1994). *A History of Christianity.* Vol. II: A.D. 1500-A.D. 1975. San Francisco: HarperCollins.

Leung, Beatrice (1992). *Sino-Vatican Relations: Problems in Conflicting Authority:1976-1986.* Cambridge: The University Press.

Leung, Beatrice and John D. Young (Eds). (1993). *Christianity in China: Foundations for Dialogue.* Hong Kong: Centre of Asian Studies, University of Hong Kong.

Li Decheng. Called to the priesthood. *Tripod,* XIV(109), 19-23.

Lincoln, Y., and Guba, E. (1985). *Naturalistic Inquiry.* Beverly Hills, CA: Sage.

Locke, L.F., Spirduso, W.W., & Silverman, S.J. (1987). *Proposals that Work: a Guide for Planning Dissertations and Grant proposals* (2nd ed.). Newburry Park, CA: Sage

Lumbala, F. Kbasele (1998). *Celebrating Jesus Christ in Africa: Liturgy and Inculturation.* New York: Orbis Books.

Luo, Yu and Wu Yin (1986). *Zhongguodalu Tianzhujiao Sishinian Dashi ji: 1945-1986 [FortyYears' Chronology of the Catholic Church in Mainland China in the Context of Selected Dates in World and Chinese History: 1945-1986.]* Taipei: Fujen University Press.

Madsen, Richard (1998). China's Catholics. Los Angeles: University of California Press.

Marshall, C., & Rossman, G.B. (1989). *Designing Qualitative Research.* Newbury Park, *CA: Sage.*

Marx, Karl and F. Engels (1957). *On Religion*. Moscow: Foreign Languages Publishing House.

McKenna, Andra Kirby Kate (1989). *Experience Research Social Change: Methods from the Margins*. Toronto: Garamond Press.

McManus, Frederick R. (1990). The Possibility of New Rites in the Church. *The Jurist*, 50, 435-458.

Mi, Michael C. Five Obstacles to Sino-Vatican Reconciliation. *Tripod*, XVI(95), 5-21.

Miles, M.B. & Huberman, A.M. (1984). *Qualitative Data Analysis: A Sourcebook of New Methods*. Beverly Hills, CA: Sage.

Minamiki, George, S.J. (1985). *The Chinese Rites Controversy from its Beginning to Modern Times*. Chicago: Loyola University Press.

Mungello, D.E. (Ed.). (1994). *The Chinese Rites Controversy: Its History and Meaning*. San Francisco: The Ricci Institute for Chinese-Western Cultural History.

Nedungatt, George, S.J. (1993). *The Spirit of the Eastern Code*. Rome: Centre for Indian and Inter-religious Studies.

The Cologne Declaration. *Origins*, 18, 633-634. (1989, March 2).

Paton, David M. (1985). *R.O.: The Life and Times of Bishop Ronald Hall of Hong Kong*. Hong Kong: The Anglican Diocesan Association.

Patten, Christopher (1998). *East and West: China, Power, and the Future of Asia*. New York: Times Books.

Pospishil, Victor J. (1996). *Eastern Catholic Church Law* (Second Revised and Augmented ed.). Staten Island, New York: Saint Maron Publications.

Plea for China – Vatican Relations: John Paul II/Message of Apology. *Origins.* CNS Documentary Service, 22, 374-376, (2001, November 8).

Posterski, Don and Gary Nelson (1997). *Future Faith Churches: Reconnecting with the Power of the Gospel for the 21st Century.* Winfield, B.C.: Wood Lake Books Inc.

Pottmeyer, Hermann J. (1998). *Towards A Papacy in Communion: Perspectives from Vatican Councils I and II.* New York: Crossroad Publishing Co.

Provost, Janes H. (1998, August 1). Safeguarding the Faith. *America*, pp.8-12.

Quinn, John R. (1999). *The Reform of the Papacy: the Costly Call to Christian Unity.* New York: Crossroad Publishing Company.

Roberson, Ronald G. (Ed). (1995). *The Eastern Christian Churches: A Brief Survey.* Rome: Edizioni Orientalia Christiana Pontificio Istituto Orientale.

Ronan, Chares E. and Bonnie B. C. (1982). *East Meets West: the Jesuits in China,1582-1773.* Chicago: Loyola University Press.

Sebes, Joseph S.J. (1978). *A "Bridge" Between East and West: Father Matteo Ricci,S.J., His Times, His Life, and His Methods of Cultural Accommodation.* Rome: Historical Institute of the Society of Jesus.

Sing Tao Daily. Daily newspaper published in Hong Kong, with North American editions.

Song, Choan-Seng (1984). *Testimonies of Faith: Letters and Poems from Prison in Taiwan*. Geneva: World Alliance of Reformed Churches, 1984.

South China Morning Post. A leading English Daily newspaper in Hong Kong.

Swidler, Leonard and Arlene Widler (1970). *Bishops and People*. Philadelphia: Westminster Press.

Sykes, Stephen, John Booty and Jonathan Knight (Eds). (1998). *The Study of Anglicanism*. London: SPCK/Holy Trinity Church.

Tang, Edmond and Jean-Paul Wiest (Eds). (1993). *The Catholic Church in Modern China: Perspectives*. Maryknoll, N.Y.: Orbis Books.

Tong, John (1999). Challenges and Hopes: Stories from the Catholic Church in China. Taipei, Taiwan: Wisdom Press.

Tripd. Hong Kong: the Holy Spirit Study Centre. (A bilingual English-Chinese journal published four times a year until 2001 with only three issues a year)

Truth Monthly. Chinese evangelical monthly paper, published in Vancouver, B.C.

Van Manen, Max (1997). *Researching Lived Experience: Human Science for an Action Sensitive Pedagogy*. 2nd ed. London, Ont.: The Althouse Press.

Wei Qingxin (1991). *French Policy Towards Missionary Work in China*. Translated by Huang Qinghua. Beijing: The Chinese Academy of Sciences.

Western Catholic Reporter. Edmonton: The Archdiocese Weekly.

Wickeri, Janice (Ed). *Chinese Theological Review*. Four issues a year. Holland, MI.: Foundation for Theological Education in Southeast Asia.

World Journal. (Chinese daily newspaper published in Hong Kong with various overseas versions)

Wurth, Elmer (Ed). (1985). *Papal Documents Related to the New China*. New York: Orbis Books.

Young, John D. (1980). *East-West Synthesis: Matteo Ricci and Confucianism*. Hong Kong: Centre of Asia Studies, University of Hong Kong.

Zhao Quingyuan (1980). *A Chronology of the Chinese Dioceses in Their Successive Bishops*. Taiwan: Window Press.

Zhang, John B. Shijiang (1997) Toward a Wider Reconciliation: A Cultural-Theological Reflection Within the Church in China. *East Asian Pastoral Review*, 34 (1 & 2), pp. 1-166.

PART TWO

CASE STUDY OF CULTURAL ACCOMMODATION

Matteo Ricci and the Jesuit Mission in China
1583-1742

EPISODE ONE

WESTERN EUROPE DURING THE RENAISSANCE AND THE AGE OF EXPLORATION

For us to better understand the person of Matteo Ricci, we will have to know his background in Europe during the 16th and 17th centuries.

Three important events stood out during this period of history: (A) geographic explorations and discoveries (B) the Reformation (C) the Renaissance.

Geographic Explorations and Discoveries

When Matteo Ricci was born on October 6th, 1552 in Macerata, Italy (1) the 16th Century had been witnessing the age of voyages and geographic explorations chiefly by Portugal and Spain. One must not forget that during the preceding Middle Ages Portugal and Spain were conquered by the Islamic Arabs. After a long and bitter struggle to free them from foreign political and religious control, the various small states gradually merged together to form today's Portugal and Spain. Nevertheless, the Portuguese and Spanish nobles continued to cherish antagonism and contempt of anything that was Moslem or religiously foreign to them, including such believers. They had already gotten into a habit of resolving religious differences by violent means, one example being the Inquisition which was strongly carried out especially in Spain.

Although the Crusades were already over, the spirit still remained high in both countries. Small wonder they looked to the high sea for possible territorial expansions. The Portuguese in particular had the multiple objectives of snatching from the Arabs the trade with China by attacking their vessels on the Indian Ocean. They also encircled Moslem countries on the Mediterranean shores for possible assaults, and to find more lands for the King's crusaders to conquer and divide up. Vasco da Gama was able to sail around the Cape of Good Hope to reach the east coast of Africa, paving the way for the Portuguese conquest of Goa on the west coast of India. They considered that such activities were extensions of the original Crusades, with both economic and religious overtones.

The Islamic countries considered the Portuguese pirates and invaders, and shared this bad reputation everywhere, including Ming China. When the Portuguese reached the coast of Guangdong in southern China and tried to carry out the 'pirating' activities, they were not able to succeed. The Ming Government was already very vigilant and well prepared to expel any armed strangers from the oceans. However, they allowed the Portuguese to settle in Macao (澳門) on the southeast coast. Thus the Portuguese were able to form a series of political and trading bases stretching from Lisbon along the east coast of Africa, Goa on the west coast of India, Malacca on the west coast of Malaya, and finally Macao on the southeast coast of China. The Pope even granted the Portuguese king "Patroado", meaning patronage of missionaries for this eastern sea route.

Spain decided to compete with Portugal in trading with China on the west sea route by financing Columbus in his exploration effort. Christopher Columbus unintentionally discovered the 'New World' for Spain. Later Central and South America came entirely under Spanish rule. Wherever the Spanish went, they forced the natives to give up their traditional culture to become Christians with adopted Spanish surnames. From their base in Mexico, the Spanish went to conquer the Philippines, then travelled to trade with Fujian province on the east coast of China, and went to Taiwan to preach the Gospel.

The rivalry between Portugal and Spain for the Chinese trade was interesting, for they both had bases in China for both trade and missionary work. They both received from the Pope the "Patroado" - the Spanish for the western route, and the Portuguese the eastern route. They both were ethnocentric and had no tolerance for native religions and cultures. Their attitude was a reflection of their mentality against the Moslems in the past in their home countries. Their evangelization in the colonies was generally supported by political and military power. It is interesting to note that "Several of the 16th century missionaries believed that if the Portuguese or Spanish king would only send three to five hundred horsemen they could conquer the whole of China and all the Chinese would be baptized.(2)

The Reformation

Martin Luther's Reformation of the church movement took place at the same time as the Portuguese first arrived in China. Before this time, Western Europe as a whole belonged to the Latin Church, commonly known as the Church of Rome. After the Reformation, the Latin Church split up, and the ensuing results were not only the birth of Protestant churches, but hostility leading to literary and military battles between the Catholic and Protestant countries over the next hundred years or so. The sad part was that the spirit of the Gospel about hope, love and toleration gave way to the rigidity of religious dogma. The emphasis by both the

Catholic and Protestant churches on their members became "the purity of faith" and the strict adherence to regulations for worship and life style.

The so-called Catholic Counter-Reformation of this time actually consisted of two important movements: (a) The Council of Trent and the implementation of its decisions. (b) The rigorous self-renewal of existing religious orders such as the Dominican and the Franciscan, and the establishment of new ones such as the Jesuits or the Order of Jesus.

In the case of the Jesuits, they had attracted over Europe many dedicated, talented and committed youths with superior family and educational backgrounds. The Jesuits became very influential in political and intellectual circles, and the result was inevitable competition from and conflict with other existing religious orders, such as the dispute over the theological interpretation of the Rites Issue in China between the Jesuits and Dominicans.[3]

The Council of Trent was a response to the attacks by the Protestant churches during this historical period in Europe. The Council vigorously re-examined the teachings of the Catholic Church such as the Sacraments, the training of its clergy, and the liturgy for the laity. New policies were thus formulated and implemented. Furthermore, the Council strengthened the authority of the Pope, and consolidated the administration of the Church. All these resulted in making the Catholic Church more authoritarian, similar to the centralized monarchy in Europe at that time, in contrast to the reformed or Protestant churches that had opted for more participation from the members at large. Nevertheless, the Catholic Church emerged from these reforms with more stability, and with the renewal of old religious orders and the births of new ones, she was able to send out more missionaries to evangelize the newly discovered lands, along the new sea routes charted by the Portuguese and the Spanish. However, the decision of the Council of Trent was very dogmatic and rigid. Naturally it would not allow for mutual harmony, or the sacrifice of authority, among Christians; nor would it tolerate the acceptance of native cultures in the evangelization process, particularly by the Portuguese and Spanish missionaries. This point is very important for us to remember as we later examine a different approach by Ricci in chapter VI.

The European Renaissance

The European Renaissance has been interpreted in different ways by different historians. In fact, it means different things to different people. Nevertheless, from 15th to 17th century Europe experienced a renewed interest in the learning of the literature and art of ancient Greece and Rome. The philosophy of that time, both in Catholic and Protestant countries, was mainly Christianized Aristotelianism, "mixed with some Platonism and certain beginnings of doubts". (4) There was a flourish of publications on the new interpretations and annotations of medieval learning, such as the thought of Aristotle and Aquinas. These new thoughts became part of the training of the Jesuits, and when some of them came to China as in the case of Ricci, they were able to use them as the basis of western learning to introduce to the Chinese, including geographic knowledge, mathematics and new scientific knowledge on the calculation of the Calendar. An example was Newton's cosmology based on "heliocentrism", combining the researches of Kepler and Galileo. (5)

Matteo Ricci was born and grew up during the age of Renaissance. When he came to China, he was fully equipped with western philosophy and scientific knowledge to assist him in his method of accommodation when he preached the Gospel to people of his new homeland - the Middle Kingdom of China.

EPISODE ONE

WESTERN EUROPE DURING THE RENAISSANCE AND THE AGE OF EXPLORATION

End Notes

1. Ts'un-ts'ui hsueh she (ed). *Li-ma-tou-yen—chiu lun-chi [Collected Essays on Matteo Ricci]*. Hong Kong:Ch'ung-wen, 1971. This works contains important information on Ricci.
2. Bernard Hung-key Luk, "The Background in European History of Matteo Ricci's Mission", *Tripod*, vol. 12, 1982, p79.
3. Malcolm Hay. Failure in the Far East: *Why and How This Breach Between the Western World and China First Began*. Belgium: Wetteren, l956, pp5-6.
4. Bernard H. Luke, *Op. Cit.*, p82.
5. *Ibid.*

EPISODE TWO

BIOGRAPHICAL BACKGROUND OF MATTEO RICCI

Anyone who attempts to study the Christian missionary history in China will never be able to omit Father Matteo Ricci, S.J., for he was the first Catholic missionary to enter China in 1583 during the European Renaissance. Cathay, as China was then known, was a land forbidden to foreigners. But Father Ricci was remembered, not so much by his success even to enter the capital city of Peking to evangelize, but by the impact of his cultural accommodation on the missionary history of the Church.

400th Anniversary of the Arrival of Matteo Ricci in China

1982 marked the 400th anniversary of the arrival of Matteo Ricci in China. At the conclusion of the "International Convention of Ricci Studies" held on October 25, 1982 at the Pontifical Gregorian University in Rome where Ricci had received his scientific education, Pope John Paul II called Father Ricci a "bridge" between the European and the Chinese civilizations, and a representation of the fulfilment of the dream of St. Francis Xavier, who thirty years earlier in December 1552, was not far from the doorstep of China, but had died on a small island within sight of this great nation.(1) Francis Xavier did not realize that his ambition of entering China during the height of the European Renaissance was later fulfilled by Matteo Ricci, who was born less than two months before his death. They both belonged to the Order of Jesus (the Jesuits), and both had the high hope that one day they would enter China and bring the Gospel message to its people with affection and understanding.

The Pontifical Gregorian University was not the only institution to mark the anniversary of Ricci's entering China in 1583. Loyola University at Chicago, Illinois also held a symposium to mark this occasion: "EAST MEETS WEST: THE JESUITS IN CHINA:1582-1773". 1583 was such a decisive date that even the People's Republic of China commemorated in 1983 in its official newspaper "The People's Daily" the four hundredth anniversary of Ricci's first step in China. For the same occasion, Taiwan even organized a large international symposium on Ricci with a publication of the proceedings consisting of one thousand pages in Chinese and English entitled *The International Symposium on Chinese-Western Cultural Interchange in Commemoration of the 400th Anniversary of the Arrival of Matteo Ricci, S.J. in China*.

Historically, both China and Europe considered themselves centres of the world. The small world around the Mediterranean called itself 'oikoumene', which meant the entire inhabited world. On the other hand, China called itself 'the Middle Kingdom', which inherently meant that China was the centre of the world's civilization. It was not surprising therefore that Christianity and Chinese culture were strangers to each other until the Jesuits came to China in the 16th century during the European Enlightenment.(2)

Biographical Sketch

October 6 1552 was an important day in the history of the Jesuit Order, for on that day, Matteo Ricci, the first Jesuit missionary, and in fact the first European ever successfully set foot on the forbidden land of the Middle Kingdom at the height of the European Renaissance, was born in the city of Macerata in Italy. (3)

Matteo Ricci came from a noble family background. His father, a professional pharmacist, was a papal magistrate and the governor of Macerata. Being the eldest from a family of thirteen children, Ricci must be very intelligent for he entered the Jesuit school in Macerata at the age of nine. He did so well in his high school years that at the age of 16, he was assigned to study law in the University of Rome.

The religious and missionary atmosphere was so high at this time in Italy that after three years of study at the College, he decided to join the Society of Jesus as a novice, a Catholic religious order founded by the Spanish convert of Ignatius Loyola as a counter-Reformation movement in 1540. The main ideal of the Jesuit Order was complete personal dedication to and exemplification of Catholicism, in particular allegiance to the Pope to defend the Catholic Church. Thus all members of the Order took the three vows of poverty, chastity and obedience. Nine months after he joined the Order and affirmed his religious motives, Ricci took the same vows and began to teach in a Jesuit college in Florence.

After teaching in Florence for over a year, he was assigned by his superior to study in the Collegio Romano in Rome. His stay at Collegio Romano became vital to his subsequent life, because his training there provided him with all the scientific and mechanical skills he needed in his entire missionary life in China. For example, he studied philosophy and mathematics under the famous scholar Christopher Clavius, who was a leader in the reform of the Julian calendar in 1582. This helped to produce our present Gregorian calendar.

Other subjects he studied included physics, the geometry of Euclid, the Ptolemaic system of astronomy, geography, mapmaking and simple mechanics. What he learned at Collegio Romano became missionary tools for him in China, where he translated most of the scientific treatises on these subjects before he died.

The Age of Discovery was also an age of Missionary zeal. The more Ricci studied the Renaissance subjects, the more he was led away from academic pursuit to missionary aspirations. As he set his vision beyond the horizon of Europe, he asked to join the Jesuit mission in India and was accepted in 1577. He first prepared himself for this new venture at the Portuguese University of Coimbra by studying theology. He then departed from Lisbon in March 1578 with twelve other Jesuit colleagues, including Michele Ruggieri and Duarte de Sande, both working with him later in China. He was later ordained to the priesthood in July 1580 and for the next four years, Portuguese Goa on the west coast of India became his new home town.

It was here in Goa that Ricci started to ponder concerning methods of evangelization. Although Francis Xavier advocated inculturalization as the missionary method in Japan and China, within the Jesuit order there was no consensus. (4) This is easy to understand because many non-Jesuit missionaries in Africa and the New World considered non-European cultural practices in religion as the work of the devil. To keep Christianity pure in the missionary lands, these missionaries particularly those from Portugal and Spain working in Mexico, Central America and South America would not support the principle of cultural accommodation at all.

In general, however, there were two schools of thoughts. One school advocated as much adaptation as possible, and the other supported limited tolerance of indigenous cultures. Ricci was thinking hard as to which course he should choose as his principal way of evangelization.

At this time, the Jesuit vicar-general for the East Indies, China and Japan was Alessandro Valignano. On the suggestion of Michele Ruggieri, a Jesuit who was studying Chinese in Macao, a small Portuguese settlement on the southeast coast of China at the mouth of the Pearl River, Valignano assigned Ricci to the China mission.

Arrival in Macao

Ricci arrived in Macao on August 8, 1582. It was the tenth year of the reign of the Ming emperor Wan Li. Of course, Europe was in full cultural bloom of the Renaissance after experience the Reformation and many dynastic wars. But late Ming Dynasty was experiencing a cultural bloom as well, more or less equal to that of the European Renaissance. They too enjoyed social security and political stability, in spite of all the court corruptions.

To understand China and for the benefits of those who came after him, Ricci's first task in Macao was to come up with a short description in Italian of the people in China, social customs, institutions and the organization of the government. In short, he made great efforts to internalize his findings so that they became his own. Michelle Ruggieri even said this in one of his letters to his friend: "We have become Chinese - ut Christo Sinas Lucrifaciamus." (5) In all his accounts, he expressed clearly his admiration and respect for the Chinese civilization.

Soon he started to immerse himself in the learning of the Chinese language in both its spoken and written form. In his letter to Europe, he said that "...I diligently gave myself to the study of the language and in a year or two I could get along without an interpreter..." (6).

Arrival in China

With great difficulty and efforts, Ricci was later able to overcome all obstacles to obtain permission from the

Chinese authorities to settle in China, " On September 10, 1583 he arrived at Zhaoqing (肇慶) in southern China, where he entered upon a long period of gaining experience, hard work, and reflection on the cultural context in which he was to perform his mission. (7)

Ricci did not come onto the scene as a Christian missionary. He knew that he had to reconcile the relationship between Christianity which was civilization of the West, to the way of life which Confucius had taught the Chinese people five hundred years before the birth of Christ. He tried to "disengage Christianity from the non-Christian ingredients in the Western civilization, and to present Christianity to the Chinese, not as a local religion of the West, but as a universal religion with a message for all mankind." (8) Ricci was well aware of the Chinese respect for learning and their willingness to listen to anything that would be presented to them in an intelligent way. Evangelization, according to Ricci, should be detached from the wrongly associated cultural superiority in this empire of high culture. His unusually good memory helped him to master quickly written and spoken Chinese. At first he dressed himself as a Buddhist monk, but he soon discovered that religion was not as respected as learning, for in China it was the scholars who commanded the highest respect in society. Then he changed to appear as a philosopher and moralist, a mathematician and astronomer, in the traditional scholar's garb. With his books, a map of the world, religious paintings and instruments of the telescope, prisms and clocks, Ricci and his fellow Jesuit companions associated themselves with the image and ideals of the Confucius scholars.(9) They learned the complicated forms of Chinese manners, old traditions and the Chinese classics. It was said that Ricci was able to recite the Chinese classics from the back to the front page, and indeed in his effort of cultural accommodation, he and his Jesuit entourage was able to win the friendship of the political and social ruling class of the educated officials. They hoped in this way that they would be able to win them, and ultimately the emperor himself, over for Christianity. Indeed, many high officials such as Li Chih-tsao and Prime Minister Hsu Kuang-ch'i became converts. With the support of the literati class, Ricci knew well that the evangelization process would soon filter down to the masses.

After living for some years in China and studying its culture, Ricci and his associates couldn't help to admire and praise the many good things in China. In the eyes of the Jesuits, there was only one matter in China which was not equal to Europe, and this one matter was religion.

With tutoring from Chinese scholars, he started immediately to learn the difficult Confucius Classics. Before long, together with Ruggieri, Ricci was able to publish a pamphlet in Chinese on the Ten Commandments. Within another few months, he put forward another publication in Chinese - a 78 page catechism entitled T'ien-chu sheng-chiao shih-lu (天主聖教事錄). In English, the translation would read A True Account of the Sacred Teachings of God. In a way, this catechism "marked the beginning of the introduction of western ideas through Chinese expressions. (10)

Putting Accommodation Theories into Practice

As stated above Buddhism was the prevailing religion in China at that time, but as Ricci wanted to show to the Chinese that he was a 'man of religion', he thought he would be better accepted by putting on the garb of a Buddhist monk. Only later was he able to find out that in China, as different from Japan, Buddhist monks were not respected much socially. He then quickly changed his dress to that of a Confucius scholar, and took up the life style as such, including keeping their beards and hairs long:

It appeared absolutely necessary that we be permitted to let our beard and hair grow, since the pattern we were following had done us great harm, causing many to think that we were Buddhists, because no one shaves except the ho-shang [Buddhist monks], who adore idols. (11).

In trying to become Chinese himself in a society of high culture, Ricci had adopted a new mental attitude to fit into his situation. In his report to Europe, he wrote the following:

I had two silk garments made, one for formal visits, and the other for ordinary wear. The formal robe, worn by scholars and notables, is of dark purple silk with long, wide sleeves; the hem, which touches my feet, has a border of bright blue silk half a palm in width and the sleeves and collar, which drops to the waist, are trimmed in the same way...The Chinese wear this costume on the occasion of visits to persons with whom they are not well-acquainted, formal banquets, and when calling on officials. Since persons receiving visitors dress, in accordance with their rank, in the same way, my prestige is greatly enhanced [by this custom] when I go visiting. (12)

Ricci also followed the other principles of Francis Xavier - that as a missionary, he should be both an intellectual and a scientist, and that he should try to convert people of upper social class in a country where people of authority were the examples and the norm. Thus Ricci mingled with high officials and to try to impress them by his scientific knowledge and instruments which he had brought along. He was always careful, however, to let the Chinese keep their ego. For example, he deliberately redrew the map of the world so that China and East Asia would stand in the centre, with other continents such as Europe, Africa and the Americas surrounding. He did so because the Chinese throughout history had considered themselves situated at the centre of the world; hence China called itself the Middle Kingdom. He called his map Shan-hai hu-ti ch'uan t'u (A Complete Illustrated World Map). (13)

Ricci presented this version of his world map to the magistrate of Zhaoqing who was so pleased that he allowed Ricci and the other Jesuits, all-be-it foreigners, buy a piece of land and build a church in Western style. His map became so popular that high officials throughout the country kept sending requests for a copy. As Ricci recalled, this annotated world map "was printed time and time again and circulated throughout all China, winning for us much credit." (14)

In Ming China, Ricci was amazed, and in fact impressed, to discover that virtually the entire country was administered by Confucius scholars, and not by the King and his relatives as was the case in some aristocratic European countries of his time. To be a civil official in China, the person must hold a government examination degree on Confucius Classics. There were three degrees corresponding to the European baccalaureate, licentiate and doctorate.

The more Ricci learned about the influence of the literati class, the more he was eager to get to know some of the scholars himself. With great efforts, tact and patience, he gradually made himself known to the people who were curious about western knowledge, science, mathematics and scientific instruments including the clocks. By word of mouth, the news about this small group of western 'men of religion' spread far and wide.

Eventually Ricci was successful in making inroads to connect himself with some of the literati and the high officials of the Ming administration. Ch'u T'ai-su, son of an influential Ming official, was his first important friend in the literati circle. With Ch'u, Ricci was able to translate the first part of Euclid's Elements of Geometry in 1607. This Chinese version was entitled Chi-ho yuan-pen (幾何v本) and was the first landmark of Chinese translation of western science and thoughts. In fact, Ch'u and Ricci had formed a study team of their own: Ricci taught Ch'u arithmetic, Clavius' scientific ideas, the making of sun-dials, the measuring of heights and distances by instruments, and Ch'u helped Ricci to learn the Chinese Classics and introduced him to other important literati in the government bureaucracy.

It must be pointed out that what Ricci had been doing about introducing science and mathematics in China was unintentional, yet according to some Chinese historians, Ricci had marked a new era in the history of China - the bridging of East and West civilizations, making this period of Chinese history an exciting one. As explained by the above story of Ch'u, a number of Chinese literati had accepted not only western science, but also western thinking. (15)

As far as conversions were concerned, Ricci's progress was slow. There were only about 80 converts in the first six years. But Ricci was not interested in numbers alone; he wanted to weave Christianity into the Chinese social fabric so that the seeds of faith would multiply by themselves. In a society where people of civil authorities were at the uppermost social stratum and were being looked up to and copied, his final goal was to convert people of this scholar-elite class, and finally the emperor himself. Then China would truly come to know Christ. If China would be converted, this Middle Kingdom and "the centre of the world's culture and civilization" would exert a tremendous influence on all other neighbouring countries including Japan and Korea.

How far did he succeed in his vision? He had indeed won genuine friendships with a number of prominent literati-officials. Of his many 'Confucian-Christian' converts, the outstanding ones included Xu Guangqi (Hsu Kuang-ch'i 徐光啓), Li Zhizao (Li Chih-Tsao 李之藻), Feng Yingjing (Feng Ying-ching 馮應京) and Yang T'ing-yun 楊庭筠). Hsu, baptized Paul, was one of the highest officials in the

Grand Secretariat in the Ming Imperial Court, and was Ricci's closest friend. Without Hsu's arrangement, Ricci would never have been able to enter Peking, have an audience with the emperor, and eventually became an honorary "custodian of clocks" in the Imperial Palace. Li, baptized Leo, another scholar-official holding high position, became Ricci's co-translator for a number of western scientific works. Feng helped Ricci to see the connection between Confucianism and western ethics, and Yang, a Buddhist turn Christian, was instrumental in assisting Ricci to prepare for his later debate with Buddhist monks.

On January 24, 1601, Ricci was eventually permitted to journey to Peking the capital. He had learned to bring gifts as tributes to the Emperor. The emperor was so interested in his gifts of Christian artefacts, glass prisms, a spinet and two clocks (16) that he allowed Ricci and the Jesuits to take up residence in Peking to preach. The emperor even appointed Ricci to repair and regulate the clocks for him. Thus Ricci started a series of royal appointments for the Jesuits in China, beginning with himself as custodian of clocks to other Jesuits as royal astronomers down to 1820's during the first part of Ching Dynasty. In fact, scientific knowledge had won the Jesuit missionaries a highly visible and integral place in China, and Ricci became more convinced of his principle of accommodation. Indeed, this idea of accommodation had made Ricci and the Jesuits no longer consider themselves foreigners, but Chinese. (17)

By now Ricci had understood well that the real moral backbone of China was Confucianism. All other religious sects including Buddhism were peripheral to this core belief system. Since intellectualism and morality were integral parts of Confucianism, Ricci's goal was to gradually blend Christian moral teachings with those of Confucius, and then permeate Christian theology within the intellectual community. As Peking was the centre of Chinese intellectualism and seat of the central government, he considered Peking as his final destiny on this earth, and never left this city for the rest of his life. There he put all his efforts into translating and publishing in Chinese the most fundamental Christian teachings, and started to reach out to the scholastic community concerning Christian morality. His intellectual discussions with the Confucian scholars had established him a place in the Chinese society. The following excerpt from his associate's journal bears witness to the success of his efforts:

> Incredible is the reputation which good Father Matteo Ricci enjoys among the Chinese, and the extent to which he is visited by important personages and esteemed throughout the whole empire of China...he captivates everyone by the graciousness and suavity of his manners, by his conservation and by the solid virtue which his life exhibits. (18)

Although a trailblazer himself for the China mission, Ricci knew well he could never accomplish his entire goal during his life time. He could only sow the seeds of the Christian faith. He needed more followers. In his letter to the Jesuit headquarters in Rome, he requested not only dedicated missionaries, "but also men of talent, since we are dealing with a people both intelligent and learned." (19) Indeed he had verified Xavier's hypothesis that to win China for Christ, missionaries for the Middle Kingdom had to be men of science and learning.

What we have seen so far is only the surface of Ricci's accommodation methods. The core of his accommodation is his intellectual attempt to bridge the gap between Confucian and Christian cultures. In the Chinese society where learning was so highly regarded, Ricci had observed that the written word was far more important than the spoken word, and hence the importance of translation and publication of

Christian and western ideas into the Chinese language. As Ricci himself indicated in his journal:

> ...Literary are cultivated to such an extent that there are few people who are not interested in them to some degree. It is also distinctive of the Chinese that all their religious sects are spread, and their religious doctrines promulgated, by written, rather than by the spoken word. (20)

Surely, this was not an easy task. Not only is the language itself difficult, but the Chinese literary tradition is permeated and even saturated with basic Chinese philosophies and values. (21)

Since the Chinese do not have their own religion, and Buddhism does not refer to a creator, and furthermore Confucianism is but a moral code, exactly how did Ricci convey the concept of God to his audience? What should be the terms used for God and Christ? In short, how was he able to accommodate Christian theology to the Chinese language? When we think deeper, we will realize that for Ricci, his accommodation was not just translating Christian and western ideas into the acceptable forms of Chinese thoughts, but was more of a syncretism - he was searching for an East-West synthesis. (22).

In 1610, Matteo Ricci passed away in Peking. He had accomplished translating several important Christian tracts, the most well known and important being: Tianzhu shiyi (The True Notion of God), which was written originally by Ricci in classical Chinese, and was published in English in 1983 by the Institute of Ricci Sources in St. Louis. It was widely considered as the first western impact on Chinese, for having a great influence on Chinese science and philosophy.

EPISODE TWO

BIOGRAPHICAL BACKGROUND OF MATTEO RICCI

End Notes

1. Tripod 12, (1982): pp. 66-67.
2. Hans Kung and Julia Ching, *Christianity and Chinese Religions*. Toronto: Doubleday, 1988, p.1.
3. Fang Ho. *Biographies of Historical Figures in Chinese Catholicism*. Hong Kong: Catholic Truth Society, 1967, v.l, pp. 72-74. Also, Ts'un-ts'ui hsueh-she, ed. *Li-ma-tou lun-chi (Collected essays on Matteo Ricci)*. Hong Kong: Ch'ung-wen, 1971.
4. George Elsion, *Deus Destroyed: The Image of Christianity in Japan*. Cambridge: Harvard University Press, 1973, pp. 54-84.
5. "Pope's Address on the Work of Father Ricci in China", *Tripod*, v. 12, 1982, p. 69.
6. John D. Young. East-West Synthesis: *Matteo Ricci and Confucianism*. Hong Kong: Centre of Asian Studies, University of Hong Kong, 1980, p. 14.
7. "Pope's Address..." *op. cit.*, p. 68.
8. Malcolm Hay. *Failure in the Far East: Why and How the Breach Between the Western World and China First Began*. Belgium: Wetteren: 1956, pp. 5-6.
9. *Ibid.*, p. 7
10. John D. Young, *op. cit.*, p. 15.
11. *Ibid.*, p. 16.
12. *Ibid.*
13. Hsiao I-Shan. *Ch'ing-tai t'ung'shih (A history of the Ch'ing dynasty)*. Taipei, Taiwan: Commercial Press, 1962, v.l, p.685
14. John D. Young, op. cit., p. 15.
15. Hou Wai-lu. *Chung-kuo ssu-shiang t'ung-shih (A General History of Chinese Thought)*. Peking: Jen-min ch'u-pan-she, 1962-63, v. IV, part 2, pp. 1204-1290.
16. John D. Young, op. cit., p. 20.

17. George Dunne. *Generation of Giants: the Story of the Jesuits in China in the Last Decades of the Ming Dynasty.* Notre Dame: the University Press, 1966, p. 107.
18. John D. Young, *op. cit.*, p. 21.
19. *Ibid.*
20. *Ibid.*, p. 22.
21. Arthur Wright. *Studies in Chinese Thought.* Chicago: The University Press, 1953, pp. 287-302.
22. This is the main theme of John D. Young (*op. cit.*)

EPISODE THREE

RICCI'S METHOD OF HARMONIZING CONFUCIANISM WITH CHRISTIANITY

With his efforts of acculturation, Ricci had gained an insight about the Chinese world-view. To Ricci, the Chinese ideology was a global one in which science, technology, ethics and philosophy formed an organic whole. For Christianity to be accepted by the Chinese, he realized he had to present it in a similar global and world-view. Such worldview was called by his literati friends and converts 'western learning'. With all these in mind, Ricci did not at first build a church, but preferred to teach in a private academy, as this was the normal and popular thing to do. Private academies teaching neo-Confucianism had been the 'in-thing' in China since the Sung Dynasty. At first, he did not want to introduce the mysteries of the Christian faith such as the Trinity and Incarnation. He rather preferred to talk about what the Chinese could relate to - such as God (T'ien-chu 天主) the creator of heaven and earth, the immortality of the soul, the reward of good and punishment of evil, and the false idea of reincarnation. Ricci believed that in his missionary effort, Christian rituals and ceremonies were not of top priority.

However, the idea of an almighty and omnipotent God is absent in Chinese and most Eastern philosophies. Ricci studied the Chinese Classics carefully, and discovered that the Chinese had the notion of God in the classical age of Confucius. God was referred to as shang-ti (上帝) and sometimes as T'ien. This idea of the Lord-on-High was lost during the Ming dynasty when Neo-Confucianism became prevalent. Ricci always based his arguments on the quotations from the Classics, especially from the Doctrine of the Mean (Zhong-yong/Chung-yung 中庸) Book of Poetry (Shi-jing/Shih ching詩經), and the Book of Rites (Li chi禮記).

In Chinese Ricci wrote the book "T'ien-chu shih-i" (天主實義) In English the title reads: The True Idea of the Lord of Heaven. In his book, he showed that in the original Confucian texts (i.e. before Neo-Confucianism) there were the basic forms of the Christian concept of God and life after death. (1)

In explaining that the spiritual concepts of T'ien (天) and Lord-on-High were inter-changeable, and that the concept of Li or Principle (理) in Neo-Confucianism was wrong, he said the following:

> I have given the problem much thought. I think it is proper to use T'ien (天) to mean shang-ti (上帝), the Lord-on-High. After all, T'ien means one vastness...Li (理), as Principle, is not the creator of all things. Thus the designation of the term Lord-on-High to meaning the Christian God is rather clear. (2)

Here Ricci was rejecting the Neo-Confucian belief that all things in the universe were part of the continuous extension of the Li, a belief that man could become one with the universe. In the Neo-Confucian cosmogony, Li begot the phenomena of yin and yang, and subsequently the five elements, before the four seasons and other living things came into existence. Ricci had to point out the difference he observed between the Christian hierarchy of God-man and the Neo-Confucian qi (ch'i 氣). According to the teaching of ch'i, a person's spirit (hun魂) would leave the body after death to become part of ch'i. In the total Neo-Confucian cosmology, yin and yang were the principal ch'i. (3)

Thus he had to point out to the Chinese that the idea of 'soul' was mentioned in the same Classics. There were passages about people worshipping ghosts and spirits, but not the ch'i. (4). He quoted the story of King Wen (Wen Wang) from the Classic of Documents Shujing(Su ching書經) to illustrate that there was a soul in each person: "King Wen is on high; Oh, bright is he in heaven. King Wen ascends and descends, from the left and right of ti (Lord). (11) After explaining the scientific function of qi /ch'i as air (氣), Ricci told the Neo-Confucian literati that it was actually one of the four elements. (5)

Furthermore, instead of debating the Confucian ethic of graded love according to the "five relationships", Ricci and his followers maintained that Christianity would make Confucianism more perfect -not just its cosmology but also its ethics and moral principles." (6) Confucius had once said that a man of humaneness (仁者) loves all others. (7) God loves all men without distinction, and if one really loves God, then it becomes impossible not to love all men. Ricci's reasoning was that if the Chinese could understand the concept of God, then they would be truly changed into men of virtue. This is what is meant by the "complementary role" of Christianity to Confucianism.(8) In theological terms, Ricci and his people wanted to start with 'praeambula fidei', with the help of original Confucianism.

In fact, soon after he entered China, Matteo Ricci was impressed by the Confucian ideal of a gentleman (chun-tzu 君子) and the emphasis of ethics in the Chinese civil examination. He later discovered by his contact with officials and scholars that Christianity must be presented to the Chinese as a moral philosophy. He was fully aware that in China which valued moral principles above all other things, it was not adequate to present Christianity as a faith-system which promised a rewarding after-life. He strongly believed that once the worship of God replaced Neo-Confucian metaphysical ideas of li and ch'i, the orthodox Confucian teachings such as filial piety, reciprocity (shu恕) and personal virtues (de/te 德) would fit well in Christianity. "Confucian culture was too embedded to be displaced by Christianity," he observed. (9)

Indeed Ricci was careful about the discussion of original sin with his converts who were mostly literati. It would be unwise to tell the Chinese scholars that they were all born in sin. (10) Instead, he emphasized Confucian virtue (de/te德) being the same as goodness, and goodness was the opposite of sin.

As mentioned earlier, Ricci saw the manifestation of God in ancient Confucian classics, and considered the Confucian Five Cardinal Relations (wu-lun五倫) - those between ruler and subject, father and son, husband and wife, brother and brother, and friend and friend - as fundamental Christian values. Therefore in his judgment Christianity was compatible with the Confucian canon, and as far as ethics were concerned, a Christian society could also be a Confucian one.

Ricci's explanation of his celibacy showed his skilful handling of an issue. According to Confucius, there are three things which are not filial, but the greatest of them is to have no posterity (pu-hsiao yu-san, wu-hou wei-ta不孝有三, 無後為大). (11) Ricci argued that this specific teaching on filial piety was not the original idea of Confucius:

> Confucius is China's greatest sage. The Chung-yung (Doctrine of the Mean中庸) and Lun-yu (The analects 論語) explain in detail his teachings on filial piety. Why is it that this great injunction on filial piety (to have descendants) was not handed down by his grandsons or imme-

diate disciples, but by Mencius? Confucius regarded Po I and Shu Chi (12th c. B.C.) as men of virtues, and Pi Kan as one of the three most humane men of Yin...their virtues are perfect. (Since all three men did not have descendants) what Mencius regarded as unfilial, Confucius believed to be of ren/jen (仁). Did they not contradict each other? (12)

Ricci considered Confucius' teachings were either partially forgotten or misunderstood through the ages; he therefore concluded that Confucian ren/jen (仁) was not quite adequate to keep man from sinfulness. Only the love of God could ensure that men would love each other. His rationale was that if you loved God, you would love humanity. After all, Confucius taught that a man of humanity loves others.

The meaning of jen can perhaps be exhausted by two expressions: To love God [and] to regard him as superior to all. To practice these two [attitudes], one would be able to possess all virtues. These two expressions, however, are actually one. If one loves another person, one also loves what this man cherishes. God loves mankind [with no differentiation], and if one really loves God, is it possible, then, not to love mankind? (13)

Ricci even went further to show that the love of God was far more important than the love for one's parents. According to Ricci, "although one's parents are dearest to oneself, compared with God, they are only secondary." (14) Ricci explained that every person had three fathers (fu 父) in the universe; they were God, one's monarch, and one's natural father. He stressed that God was the great parent, the kung-fu (common father 公父):

> The monarch's relationship to oneself is that of lord and subject. The relationship of the family master to oneself is

that of father and son. But when compared to the relationship of God as the common father, all earthling's relationships of lord and subject, father and son, are equal to the relationship of brothers [among brothers]. (15)

Ricci no doubt was successful in making inroads among the Confucius literati. One of them was Hsu Kuang-ch'i [Paul] who later, after his baptism, became a high official of the imperial court. He was convinced that Christianity could make Confucianism more perfect for its cosmology and its ethics and moral principles, mainly because Ricci was able to blend the two concepts together. It can now be seen that "Ricci's synthesis of Confucian ethics and Christian morality was by no means a simple act of blending them together... Even more important, this total syncretic attempt cannot be understood if his perfecting of Confucianism is interpreted simply as a tactic, part of the policy of accommodation." (16)

According to Ricci, Confucius' teachings were meaningful in the Christian context because they emphasized self-cultivation and the individual's spiritual attainment. (17) Although he strongly preached the Christian concepts of love, Ricci never stated that they could replace Confucius' moral principles. On the contrary, "in the process of proselytizing the Confucian scholars, Ricci had given a Confucian form to his Christianity." (18)

It is true that the methods of Matteo Ricci and his Jesuit missionaries were less existential than objective, less theological than philosophical, and in order to convince the Chinese, quite often they reinterpreted the Chinese classics in order to make their point, employing at the same time the scholastic-Thomistic philosophy. Eventually, Ricci's pedagogical and diplomatic adaptation met opposition from all sides, especially from home. Matteo Ricci did not live to see all these oppositions. He died in 1610.

EPISODE THREE

RICCI'S METHOD OF HARMONIZING CONFUCIANISM WITH CHRISTIANITY

End Notes

1. Lancashire, Douglas and Peter Hu Kuo-Chen, S.J. Trans. *The True Idea of the Lord of Heavens*. St. Louis: 1985. Ideas from various parts of the book.
2. Li-ma-tou [Matteo Ricci]. *T'ien-chu shih-i (The True Doctrine of the Master of T'ien)*; with an introduction by Rev. Lucas Liu. Taipei: Kuang-ch'i, 1966, Shang-chuan, p. 21.
3. *Ibid.*, p. 41b-42
4. James Legge, trans., *The Chinese Classics*, vol. IV: *Shu Ching (Classic of Documents)*. Hong Kong: The University Press, 1961, reprint edition, p. 427-8.
5. *Li-ma-tou*, op. cit., p. 45b-46.
6. John D. Young. *East-West Synthesis: Metteo Ricci and Confucianism*. Hong Kong: The University Press, 1980, pp. 4-5.
7. James Legge, *op. cit.*, vol. 1, pp. 6-10.
8. Young, *op. cit.*, pp. 46-47.
9. David E. Mungello. *Leibniz and Confucianism: The Search for Accord*. Honolulu: The University Press, 1977, p. 12
10. Li-ma-tou, *op. cit.*, p. 46-47b.
11. *Ibid.*, p. 63.
12. *Ibid.*, p. 48.
13. *Ibid.*, p. 46.
14. *Ibid.*, p. 43b-44a
15. *Ibid.*, p. 65a-b.
16. Young, *op. cit.*, p. 49.
17. Fung Yu-lan. *Chinese Philosophy*, vol. II, pp. 558-562.
18. Young, *op. cit.*

EPISODE FOUR

CHRISTIANITY MEETS CONFUCIANISM

In previous chapters we have discussed that there were several strong forces that shaped the Chinese world-view up to the beginning of the Twentieth Century. These were (a) ethnocentrism in the sense of cultural superiority - that China represented the centre of world's culture, hence the name Middle Kingdom with its associated anti-foreignism and xenophobia (b) the syncretism of different belief systems into an integrated one, mainly Taoism, Buddhism and Shamanism and (c) the all-embracing Confucian definition of the human order and the universe, and the Neo-Confucian belief in the unity of man with t'ien-ti (heaven and earth) among the literati.

Clearly when Ricci and his fellow Jesuits introduced the idea of the existence of an almighty deity and the creation of the universe, as well as theologies of original sin, the doctrine of the trinity, the idea of heaven and hell, the concept of morality and life after death, they were indeed challenging the traditional beliefs that had existed for over four thousand years in China. Such challenge was interpreted by many as a threat to the whole civilization of China, and the traditionalists readily stood up to defend the status quo by attacking the teachings of Ricci. This was best demonstrated in the collection of writing known as the *P'o-hsieh chi (An anthology of Writings Exposing Heterodoxy)* (1) and resulted in the first Anti-Christian persecution to wipe out the so-called heterodox elements in the Nan-ching chiao-an (Nanking 'incident') (2)

God the Creator

The following excerpts from the P'o-hsieh chi illustrates the ideological conflicts between a Christian God, and the Neo-Confucian belief in the unity of man with nature as one entity known as the principles of the Supreme Ultimate (the unity of mind, heaven and earth). The teaching of the Jesuits was indeed openly challenging the Neo-Confucian tradition:

> ...Their teaching tells us about a God who has created t'ien and ti [heaven and earth], man and all other things. [They say] His body is every-where, he knows everything and he can do all things. Furthermore, he has given man a soul (ling-hun) known [in China] as Nature (hsing). [They claim that] it would be wrong to say that Nature is t'ien, or T'ien is our mind (hsin). T'ien and ti are like the structure of a palace (kung-t'ien) and the sun and moon are like a lantern (ten-lung). Therefore, it would be wrong to say that t'ien-ti is God. T'ien-ti, God, and man are three separate matters... (3) Their teachings suggest that if the Supreme Ultimate means li, then it is not the creator of all things. Li exists only by depending on other matters. It does not possess its own spiritual nature (ling-chueh) and therefore it is not an object dependant on itself (tzu-li) (4)

We have earlier pointed out that after going back to the original source of Confucius teachings, Matteo Ricci discovered that earlier Chinese had believed in a God known as Shang-ti or Lord of Heaven, and that Shang-ti was worshipped during agricultural festivals. However, through the ages, men had forgotten this Lord of Heaven, and simply used the term Heaven to mean this God. But Heaven was not God, it was a creation of God, and in Chinese terms, God is the Master-of-T'ien. Inevitably, Ricci soon became the prime target of Neo-Confucians for pointing out that ancient Chinese had worshipped this Christian God, and that this "Master-of-T'ien is responsible for the existence of T'ien [heaven]-Ti [earth] and all things. He is completely impartial (ta-kung) to all men, and he constantly looks after and nourishes them". (5)

The idea of a creator was no doubt difficult to accept by the neo-Confucians, but equally difficult to accept was Yeh-su [Jesus] as the son of God. The following excerpt illustrates very well the Confucian idea that good must come from good, and bad from bad:

> ...In their writings [on Christianity] they acknowledge openly that the Master-of-T'ien was born sometimes during the reign of Emperor Ai of the Han dynasty. His [Jesus] mother's name was Mary and they belonged to one of the tribes of the Western barbarians. He [Jesus] was crucified on a cross by some corrupt officials. But, how could a criminal be the Master-of-T'ien [Lord-on-High]? (6)

Even the picture of Jesus aroused xenophobia among the opponents of Ricci. "One Chiang Te-ching commented that 'even if there were a portrait for T'ien, it would not be one of a picture of someone [Jesus] with a high nose, deep eyebrows and a bearded mouth' (7)

Some opponents found the virgin birth of Jesus beyond reason, and considered a religion glorifying the immoral act of an unmarried woman atrocious:

> ...Their ancestors is known as Hsien-shih-hsi [St. Joseph?] and the mother of Jesus is a Hsien-chiao-ma-li [St. Mary]. She gave birth to a son by the name of Liao [Nazareth?] before she was even married...By fifteen he [Jesus] had already possessed demonic abilities. He travelled widely, trying to persuade others to follow his evil practices... some righteous people captured him and crucified him... his followers created the story that he arose from the dead after three days...](8)

The doctrine of the original sin was also puzzling to the mind of the Confucius Chinese. Referring to God's punishment of Adam and Eve for being disobedient, some pointed out that the punishment was severe and unjust, and that in Buddhism, samsara was a punishment for a person's own deeds, and not for his posterity. "After all, an ordinary person had limited intelligence; he could easily be tempted by a demon. Why then had God allowed this evil spirit to affect the fate of all mankind? ... [And] if God's original intention was to provide a paradise for his children, why had he allowed such injustice?" (9)

Clearly according to the Confucian rationality, the consequences of one's action should never affect his descendants. And as Confucianism emphasizes one's effort to achieve perfection, Confusions found it difficult to accept the idea that God was perfect, for Adam and Eve were such imperfect beings:

> Why were Adam and Eve such inferior beings? This is like an artisan who has built an unsuited tool. We [the Confucians] would not say that it is the fault of the instruments, but that the artisan has poor skills. (10)

Equally perplexing, and perhaps considered artificial, was the doctrine of the Trinity to the Confucians. How could the "one in heaven is God and the one on earth is also God. This is incomprehensible..." (11) In Confucian tradition, God should have sent a learned man like Confucius to moralize sinners on earth, and if Jesus was an honourable person, why would he choose to die like a criminal? For nothing was as important as one's honour! Why did God choose not to descend to China? Was China, with all its history and culture, unimportant in God's eyes? "The very idea of one's fate being in the hands of a supernatural being offended the Neo-Confucians - his moral character and his relationship with heaven and earth (t'ien-ti) alone determined his ultimate destiny. (12)

Life after Death

Confucians are not very much concerned about life after death, for Confucius emphasized the importance of leading a morally righteous life here on earth. According to Confucius, what was the point of talking about spirits and ghosts when you could not even serve your fellow men here and now? Furthermore, why would not one's deeds on earth be the prime consideration for going to heaven or hell? Why would the Ten Commandments be the measuring stick? By this reasoning, what had happened to the deceased ancient sages who had led virtuous life but did not believe in the Christian God? Would they be in hell or heaven? An excerpt from the P'o-hsieh chi shows the confusion and disillusionment in the minds of the Confucians:

> According to the Ten Commandments of their teaching it is a great sin to take a concubine for the sake of having a male descendant. This means that all those emperors who have had wives and concubines were doomed to hell. I ask him [Alleni]: 'Wen Wang had many wives and concubines. What about him?'... he answered: 'I would not say this in front of others, but I am afraid Wen Wang

had entered hell.' (13) ...The Christian teaching was based completely on the commandments of God and not on the soul. For those who follow God and his teachings, their souls would stay in heaven eternally. Those who do not would end up in hell even if they were men of virtue.' (14) For the Neo-Confucians, the implication was that even Confucius was in hell. (15)

To many orthodox Confucians, the 'heterodox barbarians' of Ricci and his associates were openly defying what Confucius had taught about humanity and righteousness being the ultimate principle of living. They were teaching something that should never be allowed in China:

... [The Christians] elevate Jesus above virtues and kindness, put God above sincerity and integrity, ignores humanity and righteousness, and only emphasizes heaven. They believe that living is bondage (lei-hsieh) and death is deliverance from suffering... (16)

The Concept of Morality

Earlier we have discussed the sacred Chinese moral code based on the Five Relationships and Three bonds (san-kang wu-lun) which was linked to the Neo-Confucian cosmology. Furthermore, the Confucian concern for the present was much more important than the concern for the next life. In carrying out their principle of accommodation, Ricci and his Jesuits only accepted those Confucian rituals and practices that were compatible with Christian teachings. For example, Ricci would not baptize a high Ming official Li Chih-tsao because he was not willing to give up his concubine. (17) It is clear that the Jesuits would not compromise on matters of a more fundamental nature. The Confucian concept of morality was intimately linked to their interpretation of T'ien, but Ricci would not accept this interpretation of the Supreme Ultimate. Therefore in reality he was also challenging Confucian morality. The Confucian emphasis on a virtuous life on earth for its own sake, rather than for a reward in the next life, is clearly shown in the following excerpt of an argument:

> There is nothing peculiar about the Middle Kingdom's Confucian school (ju-men), except its jen (humanity) and i (righteousness); life or death has no bearing on the validity of jen and i. Confucius is a true sage because he mastered the true learning, and Mencius followed in his footsteps ...the barbarians knows no truth and teaches that the Master-of-T'ien is the mind; they despise this life and live emptily. They care only for heaven [for their next life]. (18)

To the Confucians, Christian teachings stressed too much about the next life, and showed limited concern for the well-being of society, or more accurately, the social order. According to Confucianism, the virtuous nature (te-hsing) of man was bestowed by T'ien and could only be revealed from within oneself, hence it is important for one to have a lifelong education or self-cultivation to realize one's potential in order to arrive at the tao within humanity:

> Thus we know the original foundation of this sincerity is nowhere and yet everywhere. Within a sage, it is known as the Way of the Sages; flourishing in all things...within a gentleman, it is known as the Gentleman's Way...Even husbands and wives can be guided [in their relationship] by following it...(19)

The core of Confucianism was the power of sincerity which could link one to the will of T'ien, and to follow the dictate of sincerity was to honour T'ien, the ultimate truth of existence. Thus, to the Confucians the Christian rituals of using holy water, ointment and public worship was far from honouring T'ien. It was, according to Confucians, by self-cultivation, particularly the study of the Classics, one could come to know sincerity and to learn to honour T'ien, the source of all virtues, and thus perfect oneself. The very idea that if a criminal would only accept Jesus, he would be saved in the next life, totally upset the orthodox Confucians; for a true Confucian, in order to honour T'ien, nothing was more important than the continuous efforts to practise sincerity.

Equally difficult for the Confucians to accept was the fatherhood of God in relation to family ethics. Ricci preached that God was the father of everyone; therefore brotherhood existed among all, including one's monarch and one's father. In accommodating the Confucian concept of fatherhood, Ricci taught that everyone had three fathers (fu) in the universe: his natural father, his monarch (Kuo-chun) and his heavenly father (kung-fu), [20] but everyone should pay the utmost respect to the heavenly father first. This teaching, however, was most difficult in the Confucian tradition:

> My father begot me, and my mother nursed me. To be filial is to love one's parents...to be loyal is to honour one's sovereign. To love one's family and to honour what is righteous are the manifestations of the nature of T'ien... Ricci only honours the Master-of-T'ien as the great father and lord of the universe...suggesting that one's family is too infinitesimal to be loved, one's sovereign too close to oneself (ssu) to be honoured; he is teaching the world to be disloyal and unfilial. [21]

With respect to Ricci's teaching of monogamy, more questions were asked than answered. Should the emperor give up all his concubines? If a couple had no male descendant, what could he do to follow Confucius teaching? (Confucius says that there is no fault so great in one's life as not to have a male descendant to perpetuate the family line).

> ...the classics say that although the female rules the dawn, what binds a family in harmony is for the woman to follow the husband, and not vice versa. ... [but] the barbarians teach that a husband should treat his wife with equal status. When the wife dies, the husband should become a widower [and observe the proper rituals reserved for a widow]. A man without sons should not acquire a concubine ...even man of noble birth [including the monarch] should not be allowed to have more than one wife... (22)

Opponents of Ricci used the following story to support their argument. A Mr. Shou Kuo-hsiang bought a concubine in his old age, but was later persuaded by the Jesuits to send her away. The result was an infant baby that Shou did not know how to take care of (23)

The Problem of Ancestral Worship

The English philosopher Herbert Spencer considered ancestor cult as the root of every religion, and many scholars agreed with him in the sense that veneration of ancestors maintained the authority of the elders, social control and traditional attitude. (24) A belief in survival after death was also widespread among Indo-European peoples from as early as Palaeolithic and Neolithic periods (25) In fact, practices of filial piety towards parents was deeply rooted in patriarchal religions among the Hebrews, Greeks, Romans and the Chinese. The Christian belief in resurrection had provided a good foundation for remembering the dead, although often they expressed such veneration in churches as opposed to the Chinese who did so within their families and clans. (26)

In Christianity, prayers and sacrifices to the dead are definitely a violation of the First Commandment, but prayers for the dead is theologically permissible. The Christian position permits veneration of the ancestors, including prayers and liturgy, but not to the ancestor cult. Such veneration was justifiably defended by The Council of Trent after the Reformation. (27)

Many scholars agreed that in China, ancestral veneration had degenerated into ancestral worship, particularly in its exterior form due to centuries of the syncretism of Taoism, Buddhism and Shamanism. In its early stage in Confucius' time, people remembered their ancestors in veneration, and all the Classics point out that Confucius himself worshipped Shang-ti or the Lord of Heaven, but refuted the existence of other spirits. In fact the Book of Rites taught that everything on earth had its roots in Heaven, and every person had his/her roots in their ancestors; the purpose of the Annual Veneration outside the capital was for everyone, particularly the kings, to remember their roots.

To this day the Chinese Ancestor Worship has the following important meanings: (a) affirmation of one's roots (Whom did I come from?). It is therefore most important that ancestors be remembered on New Year's Day, at the wedding ceremony, and so on (b) the idea of immortality: the spirit of the ancestors is present within the family among his/her children. They become a kind of guardian angels to protect their posterity (c) participation of the living with the ancestors' spirit at worship, so that when it is one's turn to leave this world, one will join the rank and file of one's ancestors.

Ricci and the Jesuits had the difficult task of deciding if this ancestor worship was veneration of the ancestors or to the ancestors. Eventually after studying all the Classics, Ricci decided, as discussed earlier, the Chinese ancestor worship was veneration of, and not to, the dead. They began to compromise by allowing the baptized Chinese to continue the practice.

However, the Chinese did not reserve the veneration of the dead for their own ancestors. They installed tablets in temples to worship the spirits of the eminent. The Jesuits were careful not to tolerate the worship of other deities such as Kuan Kung or god of war. They had thus enraged their opponents:

> The barbarians treat their parents light...going through their writings such as Ch'i-ko (Seven Ethics), Shih-i (The True Meaning of God), Ch'ou-jen shih-pen and Chiao-yu lun ...which contain thousands of words, not one word is mentioned about filial piety...not to love one's parents but to love others, not to honour one's parents but to honour others — I have never heard of such a thing. (28)

In spite of the great efforts made by Ricci and his fellow Jesuits to carry out their policy of cultural accommodation, they were confronted with monumental challenges in China, particularly in harmonizing the theological differences. As discussed earlier, the cultural setting in China was far different from other missionary parts of the world, such as Africa or the Americas. China had its own strength of philosophy long before the birth of Christ, and China was a society of learning and high culture. To ask a people with a strong belief system to accept a new religion was definitely not an easy task.

Details of how Ricci and his Jesuit associates handled the theological and philosophical differences, as well as how they attempted to harmonize the two belief systems is beyond the scope of this discourse. Ricci and the Jesuits made a concerted effort to bridge the ideological differences but had limited success. In the next Chapter, we will see how attacks on the Jesuits came, this time not only from China, but also from branches of their own Church.

EPISODE FOUR

CHRISTIANITY MEETS CONFUCIANISM

End Notes

1. Hsu, Ch'ang-chih (comp.) *P'o-hsieh chi [An anthology of Writings Exposing Heterodoxy]*, cited in John D. Young, *Confucianism and Christianity: The First Encounter*. Hong Kong: The University Press, 1983, p. 59.
2. Paul A. Cohen. *China and Christianity: the Missionary Movement and the Growth of Chinese Anti-foreignism, 1860-1870*. Cambridge: Harvard University Press, 1963, Preface.
3. Hsu, *op. cit.*, 3:8b; Young, op. cit., p. 65
4. *Ibid.*, 3:19b; Young, *op. cit.*, p. 58.
5. *Ibid.*, 5:3; Young, *op. cit.*, p. 67.
6. *Ibid.*, 1:8b-9; Young, *op. cit.*, p. 63.
7. Young, *op. cit.*, p. 66.
8. *Ibid.*
9. *Ibid.*
10. *Ibid.*, p. 67.
11. *Ibid.*
12. *Ibid.*
13. *Ibid.*, p. 68.
14. *Ibid.*
15. *Ibid.*
16. *Ibid.*
17. Some people wonder why Ricci did not consider it immoral to reject and abandon a woman whose position and status was that of a concubine. In the Chinese context, a man had to provide alimony to the concubine when he rejected her, Nevertheless, the sense of rejection made a concubine suffer emotionally. Some theologians have argued that for the Church to show charity and compassion, the Church should have allowed the

convert to keep the concubine until she died. Ricci, however, did not compromise on this issue.
18. *Ibid.*, p. 71.
19. *Ibid.*
20. *Ibid.*, p. 73.
21. *Ibid.*, p. 72.
22. *Ibid.*, p. 73.
23. *Ibid.*
24. Hans Kung and Julia Ching. *Christianity and Chinese Religions.* Toronto: Doubleday, 1988, p.
25. Mircea Eliade. *A History of Religious Ideas.* Chicago: The University Press, vol. 1, p.9.
26. Hans Kung, *op. cit.*
27. *Ibid.*, p. 38.
28. Young, *op. cit.*, p.73.

EPISODE FIVE

THE RESPONSE FROM ROME

Ricci's effort to accommodate ancestral worship was attacked by his own people in Europe. Other Catholic missionaries such as the Dominicans or the Franciscans did not accept Ricci's interpretation of the Chinese ancestor worship. They considered Ricci's interpretation a heresy, and a twisting of the fact to suit his missionary efforts. Although there is no official documentation of their logic, it was not uncommon among the Spanish and Portuguese Dominicans to consider non-Christian cultures the work of the devil, and that any tolerance of indigenous practices was a betrayal of Christian principles. Ricci did not live to see this dispute, but his fellow Jesuits found themselves in a difficult dilemma, for they had tolerated this practice for many years already.

This theological conflict eventually developed into what was known as the Rites Controversy which surfaced in 1634, when the Spanish Dominicans and Franciscans began their mission work in China. (1) As mentioned earlier, Matteo Ricci and his Jesuit missionaries had allowed the Chinese converts to venerate their ancestors and Master K'ung (Confucius), practices that were fundamental to the Chinese for over two thousand years. The Dominicans and Franciscans were offended by this veneration of ancestors, and by the use of the traditional Chinese names for God. The Jesuits were denounced in Rome by their rivals, and endless disputes took place in the Sacred Congregation for the Doctrine of the Faith. The conflict soon developed into a political issue with debates all over Europe. (2)

From the beginning, Ricci already foresaw such conflicts. On May 11, 1610, one of his fellow Jesuits asked Ricci on his deathbed in what position he was leaving them. Ricci replied that he was leaving them "before a door which may be opened to great merits, but not without much trouble and danger." (3)

In his capacity as head of the mission in 1603, Ricci had issued a directive to his mission members that the two ritual customs of honouring Confucius and the ancestors were most likely not superstitious, and therefore could be practised by the Chinese Catholics. (4) In fact, his directive was approved by his Asia supervisor Alessandro Valignano in Macao.

We can trace the origin of the Rites Controversy to the arrival of other Catholic religious orders in China besides the Jesuits. The Jesuits were the only missionaries in China for forty seven years from 1583. In 1633, the Dominicans and the Franciscans came to Fujian. These newcomers disagreed with the missionary methods of the Jesuits, and compiled a report entitled "Informaciones," describing the different views of the rites issue. This report became the basis of their appeal to Rome for a pontifical decision on the legitimacy of Jesuit methods of accommodation. (5) The Sacred Congregation of Propaganda Fide in 1645 agreed with the Dominicans, but Pope Innocent X delayed the decision of the Congregation by decreeing that "until such a time as His Holiness or the apostolic Holy See should ordain otherwise.) (6)

In 1654 when Pope Alexander VII took office, the Jesuits appealed the 1645 verdict on the rites. This time Rome supported the Jesuits and declared: "...the abovementioned rites [in honour of Confucius] ought to be permitted for Chinese Christians because it seems that it is simply a civil and political cult... [and the rites in honour of the dead] is tolerated for Chinese converts to practice the ceremonies for their dead relatives, while rejecting all forms of superstition." (7)

As customary of that time, politics was involved in the decisions of the Popes. In 1659, Pope Alexander VII established the institution of Vicars Apostolic in order to win back from the Portuguese king the control of the missions in Asia.(8) He advised the vicars apostolic in 1659 not to persuade converts change their customs, unless if such customs were contrary to the Catholic faith.

In 1693 Mgr Maigrot of the Paris Foreign Mission Society, became the Vicar Apostolic of Fujian. He was not happy about the Jesuit practice, and asked Pope Innocent XXII to re-examine the issue of the rites. The pope appointed four cardinals to study the case in 1697. (9) The Jesuits were very much concerned about the outcome of the committee, and sought a ruling from Emperor Kangxi on the question of the rites. Emperor Kangxi agreed with the Jesuit's interpretation in a royal letter dated November 30, 1700 to the Pope, indicating clearly that the veneration to Confucius and the ancestors were completely civil and political, not religious: that Confucius was venerated as a teacher, not as a god; that the veneration of ancestors was not a worship service, but a commemoration; and that the divine names of T'ien (天) and Shang-ti (上帝) did not refer to the physical heavens, but to the Lord of heaven and earth. The Emperor even took pains to explain in detail that the Chinese worship of T'ien had its origin in the actual worshipping of God according to the original Classics: because an ordinary person could only see the physical sky when he looked above himself and not God or Master-of-T'ien, out of reverence he tended to address God by its visible manifestation. In a similar manner, K'ang-hsi even compared his own person by what he was being addressed as 'the Throne', or even 'Wan-sui' (to live thousands of years).

Jokingly he said to the Jesuits he was not sure if he would live a hundred years! In their cover letter, the Jesuits assured the Pope that they were working to gradually replacing the Chinese rites by Christian practices. (10) Even this letter of the Emperor was of no use to convince Rome.

Apostolic Legations to China

The whole matter of the rites took a new twist when Pope Clement XI was elected on November 23, 1700. The next year he appointed an apostolic visitor to China as well as a commission of Cardinals to examine the issue.(11) On November 20, 1704 after a hasty study of the four-thousand-year-old Chinese tradition in less than three years' time, the commission (also known as at that time as the Holy Office of the Inquisition, now as the Roman Congregation for the Doctrine of Faith) reached the following main conclusion which was confirmed by Pope Clement XI in the document "Ex illa die": (12)

1. The word "Tianzhu" (天主) must be used for the name of God, "Tien" (天) and "Shangdi" (上帝) are prohibited.
2. The words "Jing Tian" (敬天) must be removed from the churches in China.
3. Solemn ceremonies in temples or halls in honour of Confucius or the ancestors are forbidden; however, private ceremonies before a tablet or in a private home are permitted. At public ceremonies at tombs or during funerals, a passive presence and simple material assistance are allowed, so as not to incur the enmity of relatives and friends. The apostolic Visitor in consultation with the bishops and vicars will decide on what are to be tolerated.
4. Ancestor tablets with the usual inscriptions are prohibited; but the name of the deceased on the tablets with an

explanation of the Christian belief about death alongside is allowed.

Theologian Hans Kung, in light of the late 20th Century worldviews, interpreted the above conclusion as follows :(13) Rome definitively decided

- that the ancient Chinese were idolaters and the more recent ones atheists;
- that Confucius himself was a public idolater and a private atheist; and
- that the Chinese rites were therefore forbidden to Christians.

In retrospect, we can see that Pope Clements's decree was indeed a deadly blow to the evangelization of China. As the veneration of ancestors was so fundamental to the Chinese social life, and the Confucian ethic was so basic to the Chinese social value, remaining or becoming a Christian virtually meant terminating being Chinese. "The prohibition of the rites was a decision of incalculable consequences...." (14)

Hans Kung further commented that "All in all, after the case of Luther and the case of Galileo, this was perhaps the weightiest of the numerous fallible papal decisions in matters of faith and morals!" (15)

When the papal Visitor, Maillard de Tournon, arrived at Beijing on April 2, 1705, he attempted to show the Chinese imperial court the viewpoint of Rome concerning the rites issue. Emperor Kangxi was offended by a foreigner passing judgement on a Chinese tradition:

> No one can read Chinese books, but they preach a lot of doctrine. This is really laughable. How can they presume to speak about Chinese customs and ceremonies? They preach heresy like Buddhist monks and Taoist priests.

From now on it is not necessary for Westerners to engage in religious activity in China, and we forbid it. Thus we will avoid a lot of trouble. (16)

He ordered the expulsion of Tournon, and decreed that all the missionaries must follow the practices laid down by Ricci concerning the rites. Furthermore, all missionaries must obtain permission first before preaching the Gospel.

The relationship between China and Rome was made worse when finally, Pope Benedict disciplined all missionaries who had sought out the Chinese imperial permission. He also prescribed a new oath for the missionaries to use against the ancestral worship rites.

It is rather difficult for us to fully understand why the rites issue developed into such a disappointment. Scholars have given various explanations. In the opinion of Jesuit historian Francis A. Rouleau, the Council of Trent (1545-1563) was largely responsible for this epochal tragedy. In order to prevent further break-up of Roman Catholicism after the Protestant Reformation, the Council made every effort to consolidate the past, thus making the Catholic Church "almost impervious to change". (17)

Professor Fan Hao, a Chinese scholar on missionary history, pointed out that the Jesuits and Dominicans were known to have a theologically different past. They each evangelized in different parts of China. the Dominicans with the Franciscans mostly worked among the less educated people along the coast, particularly in Fujian and Shangdong provinces; the Jesuits, on the other hand, mainly associated with the Confucian literati in Beijing and other capital cities. Naturally what seemed to be civil ceremonies to venerate Confucius or family ancestors could be viewed as superstitious practices in the southern coastal province of Fujian. (18)

We must not forget that politics and religion were in constant interplay. On the one hand the European powers of Portugal or Spain heavily used religion to achieve their political purposes. Our earlier discussion of the Patroado (the Portuguese crown) revealed that it had control of the China mission, but later Rome would like to repossess the control. Inevitably a dispute arose between Vatican and the Portuguese crown. (19) On the other hand, in China the emperor was both head of the state and head of religion. Rome must have found it difficult to accept the ruling on the Rites from Emperor Kangxi, the Pope being the head of the Catholic Church. Nonetheless, some historians such as Latourette were sympathetic with Rome under Pope Clement XI and the papal legate Tournon in their effort to unify the various interpretations and methods of the different missionary groups. (20)

Conclusion of the Rites Issue

Did the Rites issue ever come to a conclusion? The episode eventually came to an end 350 years after the death of Ricci. Pope Pius XII, soon after he was elected Pope on December 8, 1939 just before the start of World War II, on the feast day of the Assumption, made the following new declaration on the Chinese Rites: (21)

- Catholic may honour Confucius in public;
- The pictures of Confucius may be displayed in Catholic schools;
- Catholic officials and students may take part in public functions to honour Confucius;
- Bowing of the head and other signs of respect before deceased persons, their pictures, headstones and tablets bearing their names are legitimate, and even encouraged.

Again a second Vatican declaration was made on February 29, 1941 during the Second World War that missionaries and

Christians could make their own informed decisions regarding the Chinese Rites, and it was not necessary for Rome to spell out what was permitted or prohibited. Apparently as China was at war with the Allies against Japanese invasion, the Vatican would like to stand behind the Chinese Catholics, as the nation was undergoing a solidarity movement against the onslaught of the Japanese imperialism.

The theologian Hans Kung was bitter about Pope Clement XI's decision. (22) To him, the Chinese Rites issue represents a case of "genuine enculturation between liturgical purism on the one hand and carefree syncretism on the other." Although Pope Pius XII lifted the ban on the Chinese Rites in 1939 "without admission of guilt", it was "once again too late", for the "Christian God had to appear to the Asians as a completely foreign, Latin European import. Christianity became a grafted-on religion!" (23) is definitely contrary to the original intention of Ricci.

EPISODE FIVE

THE RESPONSE FROM ROME

End Notes

1. Hans Kung and Julius Ching. *Christianity and Chinese Religions*. Toronto: Doubleday, 1988, p.241.
2. *Ibid.*
3. Kenneth Scott Latourette. *A History of Christian Mission in China*. New York: Russel & Russel, 1929, p. 98; quoted by Peter Barry: "The Chinese Rites Controversy", *Tripod*, vol. 12, 1982 (Hong Kong, Holy Spirit Study Centre), p. 140.
4. *New Catholic Encyclopaedia*, New York: McGraw-Hill, 1967, vol. III, p. 612.
5. Peter Barry, "The Chinese Rites Controversy", *Tripod*, vol. 12, 1982, p. 141-43.
6. *Ibid.*
7. Ibid.
8. The mission in China and Asia were under the protection of the King of Portugal. All missionaries to Asia must sail from Lisbon in Portuguese ships, and the king had the power to nominate bishops in China. This practice came under the Padroado Agreement whereby Pope Alexander VI in 1493 divided the world in half by the Line of Demarcation between Portugal and Spain. By such a Line, Portugal had the responsibility to explore and colonize the eastern part of the world, and Spain the west, mainly Mexico and the Americas. However, Spain eventually got involved in the east - her missionaries and explorers established themselves in the Philippines from Mexico.
9. Peter Barry, *op. cit.*, p. 150.
10. *Ibid.*
11. *Ibid.*, p. 143.
12. *Ibid.*, p. 144.
13. Hans Kung, *op. cit.*, p. 38.
14. Ludwig von Pastor, History of the Popes, St. Louis, 1941, vol. 33, p. 428, quoted by Hans King, *Op. cit.*, p. 242.

15. *Ibid.*, p. 39.
16. Fang Ho. *A History of Interrelations Between China and the West.* 5 vols. Taipei: Chinese Cultural Press, 1959, p. 160-161, also cited by Peter Barry, *op. cit.*, p. 146.
17. Peter Barry, *op. cit.*, 148.
18. Fang Ho, *op. cit.*, p. 139; and Peter Barry, *op. cit.*, p. 148.
19. It was reported by CBC's program "Centre Point" on August 20, 1995 in an interview with the author of *Where Did the Angels Go?* that the local Catholic Church was highly involved in the hierarchy of the Rwanda government; the same was true of Quebec until recently when politics and religion began to separate.
20. Peter Barry, *op. cit.*
21. *Ibid.*
22. Hans Kung, *op. cit.*, p. 39.
23. *Ibid.*, p. 241.

EPISODE SIX

PERSECUTION

Matteo Ricci and later his Jesuit associates were able to stay in China from 1582 to 1717 for several reasons. First, by Ricci's method of acculturation, a warm and cordial relationship between China and the missionaries had development. In fact, a number of the Jesuits became close friends to the royal families. Second, the emperors of both late Ming and early Ch'ing dynasties were willing and happy to use the Jesuits' scientific knowledge and technical skills to advance their personal purposes. Ricci himself was the royal custodian of imperial clocks; others were royal astronomers such as Ferdinand Herbiest who was even appointed Director of the Imperial Astronomical Bureau. Fathers Ferdinand Verbiest, Philippe-Marie Grimaldi and Thomas Pereira even served as imperial tutors to Emperor K'ang-hsi.(1) Third, no politics was involved as Rome never interfered in the work of the Jesuits until 1701 when Pope Clement XI set up a commission of cardinals to examine the rites issue and sent an apostolic delegate to China to observe matters firsthand. At this point, the Rites issue in fact became a political one, for the authority of the Chinese emperor was being challenged by the Pope. The Son-of-Heaven had to affirm his absolute power and autonomy. (2)

To trace the history of the expulsion of the Catholic missionaries from China and the persecution of Chinese Catholics, we will have to go back to the reign of K'ang-Hsi Emperor (1661-1684) during the early part of the Ch'ing Dynasty.

Emperor K'ang-Hsi

K'ang-Hsi was not Han Chinese; he was Manchurian, an ethnic minority. The son of Emperor Shun-chih who overthrew the Ming Dynasty, he was taught the Confucius classics by the best scholars, yet he did not totally believe in the moralizing force of Confucianism. For he had seen many who claimed to be Confucian scholars but behaved very arrogantly, quite contrary to the Confucius teaching. Conscious of his own ethnicity, he would not limit his education to the reading of the classics; instead, he preferred personal and practical experience, and welcomed foreign learning as introduced by the Jesuits in mathematics, astronomy, and the sciences. To him, the Manchu should not be completely sinicized.

Thus, by his frequent personal association with the Jesuits, he developed a deeper appreciation of Christianity as a religion and as a western culture. (3) His worldview was not just Manchu, but included Chinese and Western. He was able to rule with an open mind, because he had the "syncretic ability" to choose the best ideas from various intellectual sources and that "his world was not confined by any rigid frame of reference". (4) As a practical man, he emphasized more on the human will than the dictates of heaven. To him, Heaven only helped those who helped themselves first, and he thus stated," When man's work is not completed to its utmost, it is impossible to know heaven's way". (5)

Such was the personal make-up of Emperor K'ang-hsi who was indeed an enlightened and wise monarch. In fact, he had developed very good opinions of the Jesuits who had impressed him not only as great western scholars and scientists, but more importantly as moralists. Consequently, he must have admired their Christian belief, for he issued the following edict in 1692:

> Earlier the Board [of Rites] decided that the various Catholic churches should be preserved. However, we allow only Westerners [not Chinese] to practice Christianity. This has been already approved. At the present time the Westerners are managing the administration of our calendar-making...in short, they have committed no crime. If we denounce Christianity as a heresy, we cannot forbid Christians to embrace it, since they are innocent... (6)

Later K'ang-hsi endorsed a ministerial memorandum commonly known as the 'Edict of Religious Toleration':

> Since we permit our people to burn incense and worship in the temples of Lamas and Buddhists, and the Westerners do not violate our laws, it seems improper that their religious teaching should be prohibited. We should order all churches in all provinces to be opened as previously. We should allow those who attend the churches to burn incense and worship as usual. With your Majesty's approval, your servants will proclaim this to all provinces. (7)

If the Catholic missionaries themselves in China were thankful for and respected this verdict, Christianity in China would have flourished. Instead, the Dominicans and Franciscans started to dispute with the Jesuits about their accommodation methods concerning the translations into Chinese of the various theological terms and ideas, liturgical practices, and particularly the Rites issue.

Initially a European concern, the so-called Rites Controversy gradually developed into a ban on Christianity in China, followed by a severe persecution of the Chinese

Christians. K'ang-hsi himself was not aware of the problem until the arrival in 1701 of Charles Thomas Maillard de Tournon, Apostolic Visitor to China. Details of this event were already discussed in the previous chapter.

The First Imperial Audience

At the first imperial audience on 31 December 1705, K'ang-hsi's tolerance of Christianity was further manifested when he excused Tournon from kowtowing before him. Soon the emperor was fully aware of the dispute among the various Christian missionary groups. He became concerned, and even taught the missionaries to be tolerant of each other:

> When you [missionaries] observed the rules of your society and obey the orders of your chief, you do not violate your [Christian] teaching. But if the Portuguese are allowed to worship only in Portuguese churches, and the French theirs, then this is contradicting the principles of your teachings. Henceforth you should simply comply with established orders and do not make any distinctions. Then everything will be in harmony. (8)

Clearly, K'ang-hsi was asking the missionaries to practice what they preached: love, tolerance and peace. Finally on June 24th, 1706 he issued another edict, requesting the missionaries to honour their religion:

> ...for members of the various societies and nationalities, since they all worship the same Master-of-Tien, they should not make distinctions among themselves. They are all under the same roof, thus should not cause any incidents. (9)

As if predicting what would happen if this kind of dispute among the missionaries would not stop, and in trying to bring about peace among the missionaries, K'ang-hsi was quoted as saying the following to the legate Tournon:

> I have nothing further to demand of you other than to state once more to the Pope that for two thousand years we have abided by the doctrine of K'ung [Confucius]; and that for two hundred years, from the time of Li-ma-tou [Matteo Ricci], and for more than forty years of my reign, the Westerners have enjoyed utmost peace in China without being guilty of anything. And if in the future, anything is done against the [Confucian] doctrines, it will be very difficult for the Westerners to remain among us. (10)

The relationship between the Vatican and the emperor took a sharp turn down slope when Charles Maigrot, Vicar Apostolic of Fukien arrived in Peking to assist Tournon. At the imperial audience with K'ang-hsi Maigrot completely showed his ignorance of the Confucius tradition; upon request from the emperor to go over the Confucius writings, he was not able to identify a single character of the classics. Furthermore, he was very tactless and arrogant in his position. K'ang-hsi was so infuriated by the whole episode that he ordered Maigrot to leave China immediately.

Tournon too, soon left Peking. When he arrived at Nanking the following year, he issued the 'Decree of Nanking' on 7 February 1707, condemning the rites of Confucius and ancestor worship. Emperor K'ang-hsi was upset by the Tournon's decree, and became disillusioned by the whole episode. To him the central theme of Christianity was forgiveness, love, tolerance and good will, but he could only see conspiracy, narrow-mindedness and intolerance among the missionaries. Two months after the Nanking Decree, the Emperor issued the following edict:

> Henceforth those who do not follow the rules of Li-ma-tou [on Chinese rites] are not permitted to stay in China. If because of these practices the Pope forbids you to continue spreading your religion, simply remain in China since you have already renounced the world. I would suggest that you stay even if the Pope denounces your continuation of Li-ma-tou's ways. If, upon reports by To-lo [de Tournon], the Pope says by your obedience you have offended the Master-of-T'ien (T'ien-chu), I will defend you. As you have been in China for so long and are already accustomed to the climate...those of you who receive the certificate [of residence] will be treated as Chinese. Put your mind at rest and do not fear... (11)

In the previous chapter we have already discussed Pope Clement XI's bull "Ex illa die"; it warned violators that they would be excommunicated. Instead of expelling all missionaries from China, here once again Emperor K'ang-hsi demonstrated his non-political stance on the issue, and his patience and care for the missionaries by the following speech which he made to them:

> Again I say, if you do not follow the rules of Li-ma-tou, the [Western] teaching preached for two hundred years in China will have to be discontinued; all Westerners will have to leave. Many times I have pointed out to you the ruinous conducts of To-lo and Yen-tang [Maigroit]. Why have you not given my views to the Pope? You have corrupted your teachings and disrupted the efforts of the former Westerners. This is definitely not the will of your God, for he leads men to good deeds. I have often heard from you Westerners that the devil leads men astray - this must be it... (12)

K'ang-his's compassion for the missionaries was further revealed when he gathered all missionaries to express his views on the rites, just two weeks before the arrival of the second Papal Legation. Definitely he was hoping for a final solution of the issue, by the tone of his words:

> From the time Li-ma-tou came to China, for over two hundred years, you men from the Western Ocean have never indulged in heterodox activities, or violated any laws of the Middle Kingdom. You voluntarily crossed the seas to come and serve under me. I, in keeping with my kindness to those from afar, have made no distinction between natives and foreigners ... the teachings you preached are of no consequence to us. To-lo, however, would only listen to Yen-tang, who did not even recognize [the Chinese] characters. How could such a person presume to discuss the truth or falsehood of Chinese laws and principles? (13)

The Second Imperil Audience

In granting his audience to the second Legation, he was very warm to the legate George Ambrose de Mezzabarba. However, after he had received a Chinese translation of the bull "Ex illa die" from the Papal Legate, his tolerance and patience ran out. The next year in 1720, he issued a statement showing his deep regret for the misunderstanding of the Chinese rites, rather than his anger against the Pope; in fact he even asked Mezzabarba to convey his gifts to the Pope and the King of Portugal:

> In reading this declaration [of the Pope], one can only ask how those mean people of the West could discuss the principles of China? They do not understand our literature and their discussions only make people laugh. The content of this declaration is identical with the heterodox teachings

of the Buddhists and Taoists. all these wild sayings are generally the same. Hereafter, to avoid further problems, the Westerners will be prohibited from practicing their teachings in China. (14)

The following month in February 1721, K'ang-hsi finally made up his mind to ban Christianity from China. The following excerpt of his edict shows his change of attitude towards Christianity and his challenge of the moral integrity of the various Catholic orders working in China:

> ...scoundrels [from missionaries] of this type are rarely seen in China; it is best if the teaching of the Western Ocean is no longer allowed in China. This way everything will return to normal and quarrels [among] the different groups will dissipate. This is the best solution. (15)

We have noted earlier that Emperor K'ang-hsi was very much impressed by the scientific and technical skills of the Jesuits, as well as by their loyalty and dedication to himself. We can imagine the disillusionment in his decision, for from now on he had to reject whatever he had accepted from the Westerners. He was particularly disappointed to see that the missionaries did not practice what they preached. Since Ricci had pointed out that the ancient Chinese already had the concept of God, and in fact had come to know him, K'ang-hsi must have asked himself the question: why would China still keep these foreign missionaries?

The Persecution of Chinese Christians

The consequences became obvious in 1717 when the ruling of the nine highest courts in China was proclaimed including expulsion of the missionaries, condemnation of Christianity, Christians being forced to renounce their faith and destruction of churches. The number of Christians shrank quickly, from a quarter of a million to a small number; those keeping their faith were mainly in the lower socio-economic class such as fishermen and farmers. A renewed persecution started a few years later, but Pope Benedict XIV was not sympathetic and in 1742, five years after the death of Emperor K'ung-hsi, issued the bull 'Ex quo singular', thus confirming the earlier decision of the Inquisition. All the evangelization efforts of Ricci and the Jesuits were definitely and completely destroyed - by Rome. (16)

CHAPTER SIX

PERSECUTION

End Notes

1. John D. Young. *Confucianism and Christianity: the First Encounter*. Hong Kong: The University Press, 1983, pp. 113-4.
2. Lawrence D. Kessler. *K'ang-hsi and the Consolidation of the Ch'ing Rule, 1661-1684*. Chicago: The University Press, 1976, p. 154.
3. Jonathan Spence, "The Seven Ages of K'ang-hsi (1654-1722), *Journal of Asian Studies XXVI*, February 1967, pp. 205-11.
4. John D. Young, *op. cit.*, p. 110.
5. T'ing-hsun ko-yen [K'ang-hsis's conversations with his sons] (n.d., preface by Yung-cheng, 1730), quoted in John D. Young, *op. cit.*, p. 112.]
6. Arthur W. Hummel, ed. *Eminent Chinese of the Ch'ing Period*. Washington, D.C.: U.S. Government Printing Office, 1943, 2 vols, pp. 327-31.
7. Wu Hsiang-hsiang: *T'ien-chu-chiao tung-ch'uan wen- hsien hsu-pien [A collection of Writings of Catholicism's Orient Mission, a Supplement]*, Taipei, Hsueh-sheng, 1966-67, cited in John D. Young,, p. 118.
8. John D. Young, *op. cit.*, p. 119.
9. *Ibid.*
10. *Ibid.*
11. *Ibid.*, p. 120.
12. *Ibid.*
13. *Ibid.*, pp 120-121.
14. *Ibid.*, p. 122.
15. *Ibid.*
16. Hans Kung and Julia Ching. *Christianity and Chinese Religions*. Toronto: Doubleday, 1988, p. 243.

EPISODE SEVEN

CONCLUSION: THE LEGACY OF MATTEO RICCI AND THE JESUIT MISSION

Pope John Paul II, in his speech at the International Convention of Ricci Studies on October 25, 1982 held at the Pontifical Gregorian University in Rome, called Father Matteo Ricci a "bridge" between the European and the Chinese civilizations. (1) In praising Ricci's effort to adapt Christianity to the Chinese culture, the pontiff even compared Ricci to the early Church Fathers with respect to their effort to accommodate the Greek culture. (2) As mentioned in Chapter I, various scholars in China also acknowledge the contribution of Ricci to the 'bridging' of the east-west thoughts. (3)

Modern historian John Young considered Matteo Ricci more than a bridge; he was the first synthesizer of the two worldviews of the East and the West, a cultural trail-blazer leading the others to follow after him, including prominent figures like K'ang Yu-wei (1848-1927), Sun Yat-sen (1895-1925), and even Mao Tse-tung.(4) Ricci as an Italian was able to show the Chinese that their ancestors had once known about this universal God in the name of "shang-ti" and "T'ien", and that the Chinese had actually worshipped this Deity at the time of Confucius; thus he was challenging the prevailing psycho-cosmological worldview of the Neo-Confucian metaphysics. Ricci went even further to point out to the Chinese that while Confucius moral teaching was good by itself and had many parallels to Christianity, itself was not perfect because it lacked God at the centre who was the ultimate love. Therefore he advocated the idea of "supplementing Confucianism by Christianity". In his effort of Christianizing Confucianism, he himself became "Confucianized"

The Jesuit Impact on Christianizing China

How great was the Jesuits' impact in attempting the Christianization of China? The impact was considered slight by some, when compared to the 19th Century Christian missionaries. (5) However, historian Arnold Toynbee was of the opinion that the Jesuits' contribution was significant:

> ...The Jesuits' approach to their enterprise of propagating Christianity in China was so different and so promising in itself, and is so much to the point to-day, that our discussion of the Asian peoples' encounter with the West would be incomplete ...The Jesuits tried to disengage Christianity from the non-Christian ingredients in the Western civilization and to present Christianity...not as the local religion of the West, but as a universal religion with a message for all mankind. (6)

In short, Christianity was presented by Ricci to the Chinese with respect and peace, contrary to the 19th Century missionaries who, because of circumstances, became a part of imperialism and colonialism.

In 1842, exactly 150 years from the Emperor K'ang-hsi's edict of religious tolerance, Europe started to colonize China as a result of the British victory in the infamous Opium War. Christian missions, both Catholic and Protestant alike, became a part of the unequal treaties forced on the people in this land of high culture. Christianising now meant colonizing, and missionaries made sure that Western civilization and culture dominated the church. Small wonder that ever since 1842, deep in the hearts of many Chinese people, Christianity has had the image of an imperialistic foreign religion, and opposition to it has become natural.

It is indeed sad that due to insensitivity and ignorance of the church hierarchy, Christianity was not able to take root in China by peaceful and spiritual means in the 16th and 17th centuries. Ricci and the Jesuits built a good foundation for Christian evangelization of China, but the foundation crumbled, not so much due to their poor workmanship, but to other human elements such as the misunderstanding and rivalry of the Dominicans and the misguided decision of the Pope.(7)

Other Contributions

Apart from their effort in cultural accommodation, what are the contributions of Ricci and his Jesuits? The answer is that they had contributed to the learning both in China and in Europe. Indeed, they had started an intellectual and cultural exchange between the East and the West.

In China, as a tool for evangelization, Ricci and the Jesuits had introduced western science and technology. Even for those Confucian literati who rejected Ricci's Christian message, they were interested in his knowledge of astronomy, geography, mathematics, and instruments such as the clock and sundials. Eminent Chinese scholar Liang Qiqiao aptly summarized Ricci's introduction of science in his book *The History of Chinese Learning in the Recent Three Hundred Years* as follows:

> Through Buddhism in the Jin and Tang dynasties the Chinese learning began to meet the Western learning.

Then, again through the study of mathematics and the revision of calendar. From this new environment changes took place in an academic atmosphere. Consequently, scholars of the Ch'ing dynasty were greatly interested not only in the calculation of the calendar and mathematics, but also in practical learning. All these may have been influenced to a great extent by Matteo Ricci and Xu Guangqi. (8)

While most writers have emphasized Ricci's contribution in China, his contribution in Europe was equally significant. Western culture was enriched with new learning from China. (9) The translation of Chinese works by Ricci and his Jesuits no doubt were significant in influencing the evolution of Western society.

For example, Ricci and the Jesuits had translated the Chinese Classics either into Latin or into European vernaculars, including the *Four Books, the Five Classics, the Great Learning, the Doctrine of Mean, and the Confucian Analects.* Ricci even compiled a Chinese Dictionary for Foreigners. Now for the first time, European intellectuals were able to study the Chinese canons and philosophy. Eastern thoughts began to influence Western thinkers, including such personalities as Voltaire, Baron de Turgot, Oliver Goldsmith, Alexander Pope, and many others. They were fascinated by Confucius emphasis on reason in the governing of China, and were impressed by Ricci calling Confucius the 'Prince of Philosophers'.

In addition to their translations, by their letters and journals the Jesuits were able to provide information to Europe on bits and pieces of Chinese living. The great debate in Europe over the Rites Controversy was a clear indication of the European passion and interest in matters of Chinese origin, such as Chinese civilization, social organizations, life styles and value systems. Consequently sinology became a subject of specialized study by European intellectuals. In a way, the Chinese culture started to confront European values, especially political and social.

When we look at the historical perspective of the intellectual dialogues between the East and West, we will come to the realization that perhaps it is less important to debate whether Ricci and the early Jesuits had failed or not. What is important when we consider Ricci's legacy is his spirit of learning, his open state of mind, and his enduring faith in both divine and human possibilities to bring about a unity that would not destroy our differences? His legacy will forever remain with us, for his spirit is still very much needed today to break up cultural and political barriers between China and the outside world.

The Relevance of Ricci

Now as we are approaching the third millennium, China remains even a greater challenge to Christian evangelization. David Suzuki once said that the purpose of studying history is not to repeat the mistakes of the past. (10) There is no denying that China has been changed or transformed by communism politically, economically and culturally. With the 'open policy' in 1978 of the Chinese government, religious freedom is said to be guaranteed. (11) Article 36 of the revised 1982 constitution reads, "The citizens of the People's Republic of China enjoy freedom of religious belief....No religious affairs may be dominated by any foreign country." Here lies the problem especially for the Vatican. It is quite clear that the Chinese government, whether now or in the future, will adhere to the principle of self-support, self-administration, and self-propagation of the Chinese church. This is part of the new culture of China. The Vatican is perceived as foreign and is thus prevented from holding dominant power in religious affairs.

Would the early Jesuit experience offer something to the bridge-builders of today? In bringing God's love to the vast population of China, should the spirit of the gospel, namely forgiveness, love and peace, come first before authority, and rigidity of rules and regulations of establishments?

The challenge to every Christian in the evangelization of China remains - how do we reconcile theology to cultural accommodation? Furthermore, as China has emerged as a world power and as politics has become an ingrained part of the culture in China, what does the Church (Vatican and Protestant included) need to learn from the religious policy of China concerning its "Three-Self" directives: that the Christian church in China should be self-administrating, self-supporting and self-propagating. All these definitely will be interesting topics for further research.

EPISODE SEVEN

CONCLUSION: THE LEGACY OF MATTEO RICCI AND THE JESUIT MISSION

End Notes

1. "Pope's Address on the Work of Father Ricci in China", *Tripod*, v. 12, 1982, p. 66.
2. "Pope's Address on the Work of Father Ricci in China", *International Fides Service*, November 6, 1982, no. 3178, p. 461ff.
3. S.Y. Chen and C.Y. Chu, "A Discourse on the Impact of the Jesuits in Late Ming and Early Ch'ing Dynasties", *Chinese Historical Research*, 1980, v.2, pp. 135-144, quoted in *Tripod*, op. cit., p. 148.
4. John D. Young. East-West Synthesis: *Matteo Ricci and Confucianism*. Hong Kong: Centre of Asian Studies, The University Press, 1980, p. 56.
5. Immanuel Hsu. *The Rise of Modern China*. New York: Oxford University Press, 1970, preface.
6. Arnold Toynbee. *The World and the West*. Oxford, The University Press, 1953, pp. 63-64.
7. Donald Treadgold, in his book The West in Russia and China, v.II: China, 1582-1949 (Cambridge: The University Press, 1973) agreed with Arnold Toynbee, op. cit., that the Pope was to blame for ruining Ricci's foundation).
8. Liang Qiqiao. *The History of Chinese Learning in the Recent Three Hundred Years*. Shanghai: The Commercial Press, 1937, p.9.
9. Pierre Jeanne, "Ricci: Precursor of Inter-Cultural Exchange", *Tripod*, op. cit., pp. 122-149.
10. David Suzuki. *The Nature of Things: Galileo and the Age of Reasoning* (Video). Edmonton: Access, 1985.

11. Jean Charbonnier. *Guide to the Catholic Churches in China*. Singapore: The University Press, 1986.

PART TWO

BIBLIOGRAPHY

Beazley, C.R. *Prince Henry the Navigator*. New York: Prentice-Hall, 1904.
Bernard, Henri. *Matteo Ricci's Scientific Contribution to China*. Translated by Edward C. Werner. Peiping: Henri Vetch, 1935.
Broderick, James, S.J. *The Origins of the Jesuits*. New York: Doubleday, 1960.
_____. *Saint Francis Xavier*. New York: Doubleday, 1952.
Bruce, J. Percy. *Chu His and His Masters*. London: Probsthain, 1922.
_____. *Saint Francis Xavier*. New York: Doubleday, 1952.
Cary-Elwes, Cluma. China and the Cross: Studies in Missionary History. London, Longman, Green & Co., 1957.
Chang, Carsun. *The Development of Neo-Confucian Thought*. New York: Bookman Associates, 1962, 2 vols.
Charbonnier, Jean. *Guide to the Catholic Churches in China*. Singapore: The University Press, 1986.
Ching, Julia. *Confucianism and Christianity*. Tokyo: Kodansha International, 1977.
Chow, Y.F.: *Christianity and China*. Hong Kong: The University Press, 1965.
Co hen, Paul A. *China and Christianity: the Missionary Movement and the Growth of Chinese Antiforeignism.1860-1870*, Cambridge: Harvard University Press, 1963.

Creel, H.G. *Chinese Thought from Confucius to Mao Tse-tung*. New York: Mentor Paperbacks, 1960.

Criveller, Gianni. *Preaching Christ in Late Ming China: The Jesuits' Presentation of Christ from MatteoRicci to Giulio Aleni*. Taipei, Taiwan: Taipei Ricci Institute, 1997.

Cronin, Vincent. *The Wise Man from the West*. New York: Doubleday Anchor, 1957.

Crystal, David. The Cambridge Factfinder. Cambridge: The University Press, 2007.

Dawson, Raymond. *The Chinese Chameleon: An Analysis of European Conception of the Chinese Civilization*. New York: Oxford University Press, 1967.

Dunne, George, S.J. *Generation of Giants: the Story of the Jesuits in China in the Last Decades of the Ming Dynasty*. Notre Dame: The University Press, 1966.

Elison, George. *Deus Destroyed: The Image of Christianity in Early Modern Japan*. Cambridge, Mass.: Harvard University Press, 1973.

Fairbank, John K. (ed.) *The Cambridge History of China, vol. 10: Late Ch'ing, 1800-1911, Part 1*. Cambridge, Mass.: Harvard University Press, 1968.

———. *The Chinese World Order*. Cambridge, Mass.: Harvard University Press, 1968.

———. The Missionary Enterprise in China and America. Cambridge, Mass.: Harvard University Press, 1974.

Fulop-Miller, Rene. *The Power and Secret of the Jesuits*. Translated by F.S. Flint and D.F. Tait. New York: The Viking Press, 1930.

Fung, Yu-lan. *A History of Chinese Philosophy*. Translated by Derk Bodde. Princeton: The University Press, 1953, 2 vols.

Groot, J.J.M.. de. *Sectarianism and Religious Persecution in China*. Amsterdam: J. Miller, 1904, 2 vols.

Harris, George L. "The Mission of Matteo Ricci, S.J.: A Case Study of an Effort at Guided Culture Change in the Sixteenth Century", *Monumenta Serica XXV*, pp. 1-168.

Hay, Malcolm. *Failure in the Far East: Why and How the Breach Between the Western World and China First Began.* Belgium: Wetteren, 1956.

Holy Bible, The: Revised and Standard Version Containing the Old and New Testaments. Prepared by the Catholic Biblical Association of Great Britain. London: Catholic Truth Society, 1966.

Hsu, Immanuel. *The Rise of Modern China.* New York: Oxford University Press, 1970.

Hummel, Arthur W., ed. *Eminent Chinese of the Ch'ing Period.* Washington, D.C.: U.S. Government Printing Office, 1943, 2 vols, pp. 327-331.

Kessler, Lawrence D. *K'ang-his and the Consolidation of the Ch'ing Rule, 1661-1684.* Chicago: The University Press, 1976.

Legge, James (ed. & trans.) *The Chinese Classics.* Hong Kong: The University Press, 1960, 5 vols.

_____. *The Notions of the Chinese Concerning Gods and Spirits, with an Examination of the Defence of An Essay on the Prior Rendering of the words Elohim and Theos into the Chinese Language.* Hong Kong: The Register Office, 1852.

Leys, Simon. *China Shadows.* New York: Doubleday, 1977.

Lo, Kuang. *The History of Catholic Mission in China.* Taipei: Fujen University Press, 1967.

O'Neill, Frederick. *The Quest for God in China.* London: Allen & Unwin, 19245

Parker, E.H. "The Term T'ien-chu", *China Review (Hong Kong)*, XVIII, no. 3 (1889-1890), p. 196.

Proceedings of the International Symposium on Chinese-Western Cultural Interchange kin Commemoration of the 400th Anniversary of the Arrival of Matteo Ricci, S.J. in China. Taipei, Taiwan: Fujen University Press, 1984.

Ricci, Matteo, S.J. *China in the Sixteenth Century: the Journals of Matthew Ricci, 1583-1610.* Translated by Louis J. Gallagher, S.J. New York: Random House, 1953.

Rosso, Antonio Sisto. *Apostolic Legations to China of the Eighteenth Century.* South Pasadena: P.D. and Ione Perkins, 1948.

Rowbotham, Arnold H. *Missionary and Mandarin: the Jesuits at the Court of China.* Berkeley: University of California Press, 1942.

Saeki, P.Y. *The Nestorian Monument and the Relics in China.* Tokyo: Toho Bunkwa Gakukin, 1937.

Sebes, Joseph, S.J. *A "Bridge" Between East and West: Father Matteo Ricci, S.J.: His Times, His Life, and His Methods of Cultural Accommodation.* Rome: Historical Institute of the Society of Jesus [1978?].

Shelley-Price, L. *Confucius and Christ.* New York: The Philosophical Library, 1951.

Spence, Jonathan D. Emperor of China: Self-portrait of K'ang-hsi. New York: Alfred A. Knopf, 1974.

_____, "The Seven Ages of K'ang-hsi (1654-1722)", *Journal of Asian Studies XXVI*, February 1967, Pp, 205-211.

Suzuki, David. *The Nature of Things: Galileo and the Age of Reasoning (Video Tape).* Edmonton: Access Productions, 1985.

Toynbee, Arnold. *The West in Russia and China, Vol. II: China, 1582-1949.* Cambridge: The University Press, 1973.

Tripod: Special Issue on Matteo Ricci. Hong Kong: Holy Sprit Study Centre, Vol. 12, 1982.

Young, John D. Confucianism and Christianity: The First Encounter. Hong Kong: The University Press, 1983.

_____. East-West Synthesis: *Matteo Ricci and Confucianism.* Hong Kong: Centre of Asian Studies, the University of Hong Kong, 1980.

PART THREE

APPENDIX

Letter of the Holy Father Pope Benedict XVI to the Bishops, Priests, Consecrated Persons and Lay Faithful of the Catholic Church in the People's Republic of China
[May 27, 2007]

Editorial Note: The First Part of the Letter concerns the theological (and therefore the official) position of the Holy See (Vatican) with regards to the Three Self Movements of the Catholic Church in China. As the Letter is lengthy, only the First Part of the Letter is included here for the information and reference of the readers so that they can make their own judgment about the Sino-Vatican relations in China today. The Second Part of the Letter concerns "Guidelines for Pastoral Life". Footnotes of the Letter are left out for easier printing as there are too numerous of them. For the original English edition of the Letter, please consult *Tripod* (autumn 2007, pp.5 – 41).

Greeting

1. Dear Brother Bishops, dear priests, consecrated persons and all the faithful of the Catholic Church in China: "We always thank God, the Father of our Lord Jesus Christ, when we pray for you, because we have heard of your faith in Jesus Christ and of the love which you have for all the saints, because of the hope laid up for you in heaven...We have not ceased to pray for you, asking that

you may be filled with the knowledge of his will in all spiritual wisdom and understanding, to lead a life worthy of the Lord, fully pleasing to him, bearing fruit in every good work and increasing in the knowledge of God. May you be strengthened with the power, according to his glorious might, for all endurance and patience with joy." (Col 1:3-5, 9-11).

These words of the Apostle Paul are highly appropriate for expressing the sentiments that I, as the Successor of Peter and universal Pastor of the Church, feel towards you. You know well how much you are present in my heart and in my daily prayer and how deep is the relationship of communion that unites us spiritual.

Purpose of the Letter

2. I wish, therefore, to convey to all of you the expression of my fraternal closeness. With intense joy I acknowledge your faithfulness to Christ the Lord and to the Church, a faithfulness that you have manifested "sometimes at the price of grave sufferings," since "it has been granted to you that for the sake of Christ you should not only believe in him but also suffer for his sake" (Phil 1:29). Nevertheless, some important aspects of the ecclesial life of your country give cause for concern.

Without claiming to deal with every detail of the complex guidelines concerning the life of the Church and the task of evangelization in China, in order to help you discover what the Lord and Master, Jesus Christ, "the key, the centre and the purpose of the whole of human history" wants from you.

**FIRST PART: THE SITUATION OF THE CHURCH
– THEOLOGICAL ASPECTS**

Globalization, modernity and atheism
3. As I turn my attention towards your People, which has distinguished itself among the other peoples of Asia for the splendor of its ancient civilization, with all its experience of wisdom, philos-

ophy, art and science, I am pleased to note how, especially in recent times, it has also moved decisively towards achieving significant goals of socio-economic progress, attracting the interest of the entire world.

As my venerable predecessor Pope John Paul II once said, "The Catholic Church for her part regards with respect this impressive thrust and far-sighted planning, and with discretion offers her own contribution in the promotion and defence of the human person, and of the person's values, spirituality and transcendent vocation. The Church has very much at heart the values and objectives which are of primary importance also to modern China: solidarity, peace, social justice, the wise management of the phenomenon of globalization."

The pressure to attain the desired and necessary economic and social development and the search for modernity are accompanied by two different and contrasting phenomena, both of which should nonetheless be evaluated with equal prudence and a positive apostolic spirit. On the one hand, especially among the young, one can detect a growing interest in the spiritual and transcendent dimension of the human person, with a consequent interest in religion, particularly in Christianity. On the other hand, there are signs, in China too, of the tendency towards materialism and hedonism which are spreading from the big cities to the entire country.

In this context, in which you are called to live and work, I want to remind you of what Pope John Paul II emphasized so strongly and vigorously: the new evangelization demands the proclamation of the Gospel to modern man, with a keen awareness that, just as during the first Christian millennium the Cross was planted in Europe and during the second in the American continent and in Africa, so during the third millennium a great harvest of faith will be reaped in the vast and vibrant Asian continent.

"'Duc in altum' (Lk 5:4). These words ring out for us today, and they invite us to remember the past with gratitude, to live the present with enthusiasm and to look forward to the future with confidence: 'Jesus Christ is the same yesterday and today and for ever' (Heb 13.8)." In China too the Church is called to be a witness of Christ, to look forward with hope, and – in proclaiming the Gospel – to measure up to the new challenges that the Chinese People must face.

The word of God helps us, once again, to discover the mysterious and profound meaning of the Church's path in the world. The fact "the subject of one of the most important visions of the Book of Revelation is the Lamb in the act of opening a scroll, previously closed with seven seals that no one had been able to break open. John is even shown in tears, for he finds no one worthy of opening the scroll or reading it (cf. Rev 5:4). History remains indecipherable, incomprehensible. No one can read it. Perhaps John's weeping before the mystery of a history so obscure expresses the Asian Churches' dismay at God's silence in the face of the persecutions to which they were exposed at that time. It is a dismay that can clearly mirror our consternation in the fact of the serious difficulties, misunderstandings and hostility that the Church also suffers today in various parts of the world. These are trials that the Church does not of course deserve, just as Jesus himself did not deserve his torture. However, they reveal both the wickedness of man, when he abandons himself to the promptings evil, and also the superior ordering of events on God's part."

Today, as in the past, to proclaim the Gospel means to preach and bear witness to Jesus Christ, crucified and risen, the new Man, conqueror of sin and death. He enables human beings to enter into a new dimension, where mercy and love shown even to enemies can bear witness to the victory of the Cross over all weakness and human wretchedness. In your country too, the proclamation of Christ crucified and risen will be possible to the extent that, with fidelity to the Gospel, in communion with the Successor the Apostle Peter and with the universal Church, you are able to put into practice the signs of love and unity ("even as I have loved you, that you also love one another. By this all men will know that you are my disciples, if you have love for one another...even as you, Father, are in me, and I in you, that they also may be one in us, so that the world may believe that you have sent me"—Jn 13:34-35; 17:21).

Willingness to engage in respectful and constructive dialogue

4. As universal Pastor of the Church I wish to manifest sincere gratitude to the Lord for the deeply-felt witness of faithfulness offered by the Chinese Catholic community in truly difficult circumstances. At the same time, I sense the urgent need, as my deep and compelling duty and as an expression of my paternal love, to confirm the faith of Chinese Catholics and favor their unity with the means proper to the Church.

I am also following with particular interest the events of the entire Chinese People, whom I regard with sincere admiration and sentiments of friendship, to the point where I express the hope "that concrete forms of communication and cooperation between the Holy See and the People's Republic of China may soon be established. Friendship is nourished by contacts, by a sharing in the joy and sadness of different situations, by solidarity and mutual assistance." And pursuing this line of argument, my venerable predecessor added: " It is no secret that the Holy See, in the name of the whole Catholic Church and, I believe, for the benefit of the whole human family, hopes for the opening of some form of dialogue with the authorities of the People's Republic of China. Once the misunderstandings of the past have been overcome, such a dialogue would make it possible for us to work together for the good of the Chinese People and for peace in the world."

I realize that the normalization of relations with the People's Republic of China requires time and presupposes the good will of both parties. For its part, the Holy See always remains open to the negotiations, so necessary if the difficulties of the present time are to be overcome.

This situation of misunderstandings and incomprehension weighs heavily, serving the interests of the neither the Chinese authorities nor the Catholic Church in China. As Pope John Paul II stated, recalling what Father Matteo Ricci wrote from Beijing, "so too today the Catholic Church seeks no privilege from China and its leaders, but solely the resumption of dialogue, in order to build a relationship based upon mutual respect and deeper understanding." Let China rest assured that the Catholic Church sincerely proposes to offer, once again, humble and disinterested service in the areas of her competence, for the good of Chinese Catholics and for the good of all the inhabitants of the country.

As far as relations between the political community and the Church in China are concerned, it is worth calling to mind the enlightening teaching of the Second Vatican Council, which states: "The Church, by reason of her role and competence, is not identified with any political community nor is she tied to any political system. She is at once the sign and the safeguard of the transcendental dimension of the human person." And the Council continues: "The political community and the Church are autonomous and independent of each other in their own fields. They are both at the service of the personal and social vocation of the same individuals, though under different titles. Their service will be more efficient and beneficial to all if both institutions develop better cooperation according to the circumstances of place and time."

Likewise, therefore, the Catholic Church which is in China does not have a mission to change the structure or administration of the State; rather, her mission is to proclaim Christ to men and women, as the Savior of the world, basing herself – in carrying out her proper apostolate – on the power of God. As I recalled in my Encyclical *Deus Caritas Est*, "The Church cannot and must not take upon herself the political battle to bring about the most just society possible. She cannot and must not replace the State. Yet at the same time she cannot and must not remain on the sidelines in the fight for justice. She has to play her part through rational argument and she has to reawaken the spiritual energy without which justice, which always demands sacrifice, cannot prevail and prosper. A just society must be the achievement of politics, not of the Church. Yet the promotion of justice through efforts to bring about openness of mind and will to the demands of the common good is something which concerns the Church deeply."

In the light of these unrenounceable principles, the solution to existing problems cannot be pursued via an ongoing conflict with the legitimate civil authorities; at the same time, though, compliance with those authorities is not acceptable when they interfere unduly in matters regarding the faith and discipline of the Church. The civil authorities are well aware that the Church in her teaching invites the faithful to be good citizens, respectful and active contributors to the common good in their country, but it is likewise clear that she asks the State to guarantee to those same Catholic citizens the full exercise of their faith, with respect for authentic religious freedom.

Communion between particular Churches in the universal Church

5. Beloved Catholic Church in China, you are a small flock present and active within the vastness of an immense People journeying through history. How stirring and encouraging these words of Jesus are for you: "Fear not, little flock, for it is your Father's good pleasure to give you the kingdom" (Lk 12:32)! "You are the salt of the earth...you are the light of the world": therefore "let your light so shine before men, that they may see your good works and give glory to your Father who is in heaven" (Mt 5:13, 14, 16).

In the Catholic Church which is in China, the universal Church is present, the Church of Christ, which in the Creed we acknowledge to be one, holy, catholic and apostolic, that is to say, the universal community of the Lord's disciples.

As you know, the profound unity which binds together the particular Churches found in China, and which likewise places them in intimate communion with all the other particular Churches throughout the world, has its roots not only in the same faith and in a common Baptism, but above all in the Eucharist and in the episcopate. Likewise, the unity of the episcopate, of which "the

Roman Pontiff, as the Successor of Peter, is the perpetual and visible source and foundation"", continues down the centuries through the apostolic succession and is the foundation of the identity of the Church in every age with the Church built by Christ on Peter and on the other Apostles.

Catholic doctrine teaches that the Bishop is the visible source and foundation of unity in the particular Church entrusted to his pastoral ministry. But in every particular Church, in order that she may be fully Church, there must be present the supreme authority of the Church, that is to say, the Episcopal College together with its Head, the Roman Pontiff, and never apart from him. Therefore the ministry of the Successor of Peter belongs to the essence of every particular Church "from within". Moreover, the communion of all the particular Churches in the one Catholic Church, and hence the ordered hierarchical communion of all the bishops, successors of the Apostles, with the Successor of Peter, are a guarantee of the unity of the faith and life of all Catholics. It is therefore indispensable, for the unity of the Church in individual nations, that every Bishop should be in communion with the other Bishops, and that all should be in visible and concrete communion with the Pope.

No one in the Church is a foreigner, but all are citizens of the same People, members of the same Mystical Body of Christ. The bond of sacramental communion is the Eucharist, guaranteed by the ministry of Bishops and priests.

The whole of the Church which is in China is called to live and to manifest this unity in a richer spirituality of communion, so that, taking account of the complex concrete situations in which the Catholic community finds itself, she may also grow in a harmonious hierarchical communion. Therefore, Pastors and faithful are called to defend and safeguard what belongs to the doctrine and the tradition of the Church.

Tensions and divisions within the Church: pardon and reconciliation

Addressing the whole Church in his Apostolic Letter *Novo Millennio Ineunite*, my venerable predecessor Pope John Paul II, stated that an "important area in which there has to be commitment and planning on the part of the universal Church and the particular Churches [is] *the domain of communion (koinonia)*, which embodies and reveals the very essence of the mystery of the Church, Communion is the fruit and demonstration of that love which springs from the heart of the Eternal Father and is poured out upon us through the Spirit whom Jesus gives us (cf. Rom 5:5), to make us all 'one heart and one soul' (Acts 4:32). It is in building this communion of love that the Church appears as 'sacrament' as the 'sign and instrument of intimate union with God and of the unity of the human race'. The Lord's words on this point are too precise for us to diminish their import. Many things are necessary for the Church's journey through history, not least in this new century; but without charity (agape) all will be in vain. It is again the Apostle Paul who in his hymn to love reminds us: even if we speak the tongues of men and of angels, and if we have faith 'to move mountains', but are without love, all will come to 'nothing' (cf. I Cor 13.2). Love is truly the 'heart' of the Church."

These matters, which concern the very nature of the universal Church, have a particular significance for the Church which is in China. Indeed you are aware of the problems that she is seeking to overcome – within herself and in her relations with Chinese civil society – tensions, divisions and recrimination.

In this regard, last year, while speaking of the nascent Church, I had occasion to recall that "from the start of the community of the disciples has known not only the joy of the Holy Spirit, the grace of truth and love, but also trials that are constituted above all by disagreements about the truths of faith, with the consequent wounds to communion. Just as the fellowship of love has existed since the outset and will continue to the end (cf. 1 Jn 1:1ff), so also, from the start, division unfortunately arose. We should not be surprised that it still exists today...Thus, in the events of the world but also in the weaknesses of the Church, there is always a risk of losing faith, hence, also love and brotherhood. Consequently it is a specific duty of those who believe in the Church of love and want to live in her to recognize this danger too."

The history of the Church teaches us, then, that authentic communion is not expressed without arduous efforts at reconciliation. Indeed, the purification of memory, the pardoning of wrong-doers, the forgetting of injustices suffered and the loving restoration to serenity of troubled hearts, all to be accomplished in the name of Jesus crucified and risen, can require moving beyond personal positions or viewpoints, born of painful or difficult experiences. These are urgent steps that must be taken if the bonds of communion between the faithful and the Pastors of the Church in China are to grow and be made visible.

For this reason, my venerable predecessor on several occasions addressed to you an urgent invitation to pardon and reconciliation. In this regard, I am pleased to recall a passage from this message that he sent you at the approach of the Holy Year 2000: "In your preparation for the Great Jubilee, remember that in the biblical tradition this moment always entailed the obligation to forgive one another's debts, to make satisfaction for injustices committed, and to be reconciled with one's neighbor. You too have heard the proclamation of the 'great joy prepared for all peoples': the love and mercy of the Father, the Redemption accomplished in Christ. To the extent that you yourselves are ready to accept this joyful proclamation, you will be able to pass it on by your lives, to the men and woman around you. My ardent desire is that you will respond to the interior promptings of the Holy Spirit by forgiving one another whatever needs to be forgiven, one another, by accepting one another and by breaking down all barriers in order to overcome every possible cause of division. Do not forget the words of Jesus at the Last Supper: 'By this all will know that you are my disciples, if you have love for one another' (Jn 13:35). I rejoiced when I learned that you intend your most precious gift on the occasion of the Great Jubilee to be unity among yourselves and unity with the Successor of Peter. This intention can only be a fruit of the Spirit who guides the Church along the arduous paths of reconciliation and unity."

We all realize that this journey cannot be accomplished overnight, but be assured that the whole Church will raise up an insistent prayer for you to this end.

Keep in mind, moreover, that your path of reconciliation is supported by the example and the prayer of so many "witnesses of the truth" who have suffered and have forgiven, offering their lives for the future of the Catholic Church in China. Their very existence represents a permanent blessing for you in the presence of our Heavenly Father, and their memory will not fail to produce abundant fruit.

Ecclesial communities and State agencies: relationships to be lived in truth and charity

7. A careful analysis of the aforementioned painful situation of serious differences (cf. section 6 above), involving the lay faithful and their Pastors, highlights among the various causes the significant part played by agencies that have been imposed as the principal determinants of the life of the Catholic community. Still today, in fact, recognition from these agencies is the criterion for declaring a community, a person or a religious place legal and therefore "official". All this has caused division both among the clergy and among the lay faithful. It is a situation primarily dependent on factors external to the Church, but it has seriously conditioned her progress, giving rise also to suspicions, mutual accusations and recriminations, and it continues to be a weakness in the Church that causes concern.

Regarding the delicate issue of the relations to be maintained with the agencies of the State, particular enlightenment can be found in the invitation of the Second Vatican Council to follow the words and modus operandi of Jesus Christ. He, indeed, "did not wish to be a political Messiah who would dominate by force but preferred to call himself the Son of Man (Mk 10:45). He showed himself as the perfect Servant of God who 'will not break a bruised reed or quench a smoldering wick' (Mt 12:20). He recognized civil authority and its rights when he ordered tribute to be paid to Caesar, but he gave clear warning that the greater rights of God must be respected: 'Render therefore to Caesar the things that are Caesar's, and to God, the things that are God's' (Mt 22.21). Finally, he brought his revelation to perfection when he accomplished on the Cross the work of redemption by which he achieved salvation and true freedom for the human race. For he bore witness to the truth but refused to use force to impose it on those who spoke out against it. His Kingdom does not establish its claims by force, but is established by bearing witness to and listening to the truth and it grows by the love with which Christ, lifted up on the Cross, draws people to himself (cf. Jn 12:32)".

Truth and charity are the two supporting pillars of the life of the Christian community. For this reason, I have observed that "the Church of love is also the Church of truth, understood primarily as fidelity to the Gospel entrusted by the Lord Jesus to his followers... However, if the family of God's children is to live in unity and peace, it needs someone to keep it in the truth and guide it with wise and authoritative discernment: this is what the ministry of the Apostles is required to do. And here we come to an important point. The Church is wholly of the Spirit but has a structure, the apostolic succession, which is responsible for guaranteeing that the Church endures in the truth given by Christ, from whom the capacity to love also comes...The Apostles and their successors are therefore the custodians and authoritative witnesses of the deposit of truth consigned to the Church, and are likewise the ministers of charity. These are two aspects that go together...Truth and love are the two faces of the same gift that comes from God and, thanks to the apostolic ministry, is safeguarded in the Church and handed down to us, to our present time!"

Therefore the Second Vatican Council underlines that "those also have a claim on our respect and charity who think and act differently from us in social, political, and religious matters. In fact, the more deeply, through courtesy and love, we come to understand their ways of thinking, the more easily will we be able to enter into dialogue with them". But, as the same Council admonishes us, "love and courtesy of this kind should not, of course, make us indifferent to truth and goodness."

Considering "Jesus' original plan", it is clear that the claim of some agencies, desired by the State and extraneous to the structure of the Church, to place themselves above the Bishops and to guide the life of the ecclesial community, does not correspond to Catholic doctrine, according to which the Church is "apostolic", as the Second Vatican Council underlined. The Church is apostolic "in her origin because she has been built on 'the foundation of the Apostles' (Eph 2:20). She is apostolic in her teaching which is the same as that of the Apostles. She is apostolic by reason of her structure insofar as she is taught, sanctified, and guided until Christ returns by the Apostles through their successors who are the Bishops in communion with the Successor of Peter." Therefore, in every individual particular Church, "it is in the name of the Lord that the diocesan Bishop [and only he] leads the flock entrusted to him, and he does so as the proper, ordinary and immediate Pastor", at a national level, moreover, only a legitimate Episcopal Conference can formulate pastoral guidelines, valid for the entire Catholic community of the country concerned.

Likewise, the declared purpose of the aforementioned agencies to implement "the principles of independence and autonomy, self-management and democratic administration of the Church" is incompatible with Catholic doctrine, which from the time of the ancient Creeds professes the Church to be "one, holy, catholic and apostolic"..

In the light of the principles here outlines, Pastors and lay faithful will recall that the preaching of the Gospel, catechesis and charitable activity, liturgical and cultic action, as well as all pastoral choices, are uniquely the competence of the Bishops together with their priests in the unbroken continuity of the faith handed down by the Apostles in the Sacred Scriptures and in Tradition, and therefore they cannot be subject to any external interference.

Given this difficult situation, not a few members of the Catholic community are asking whether recognition from the civil authorities – necessary in order to function publicly – somehow compromises communion with the universal Church. I am fully aware that this problem causes painful disquiet in the hearts of Pastors and faithful. In this regard I maintain, in the first place, that the requisite and courageous safeguarding of the deposit of faith and of sacramental and hierarchical communion is not of itself opposed to dialogue with the authorities concerning those aspect of the life of the ecclesial community that fall within the civil sphere. There would not be any particular difficulties with acceptance of the recognition granted by civil authorities on the condition that this does not entail the denial of unrenounceable principles of faith and of ecclesiastical communion. In not a few particular instances, however, indeed almost always, in the process of recognition of intervention of certain bodies obliges the people involved to adopt attitudes, make gestures and undertake commitments that are contrary to the dictates of their conscience as Catholics. I understand, therefore, how in such varied conditions and circumstances it is difficult to determine the correct choice to be made. For this reason the Holy See, after restating the principles, leaves the decision to the individual Bishop who, having consulted his presbyterate, is better able to know the local situation, to weigh the concrete possibilities of choice and to evaluate the possible consequences within the diocesan community. It could be that the final decision does not obtain the consensus of all the priests and faithful. I express the hope, however, that it will be accepted, albeit with suffering and that the unity of the diocesan community with its own Pastor will be maintained.

It would be good, finally, if Bishops and priests, with truly pastoral hearts, were to take every possible step to avoid giving rise to situations of scandal, seizing opportunities to form the consciences of the faithful, with particular attention to the weakest: all this should be lived out in communion and in fraternal understanding, avoiding judgments and mutual condemnations. In this case too, it must be kept in mind, especially where there is little room for freedom, that in order to evaluate the morality of an act it is necessary to devote particular care to establishing the real intentions of the person concerned, in addition to the objective shortcoming. Every case, then, will have to be pondered individually, taking account of the circumstances.

The Chinese Episcopate

8. In the Church – the People of God – only the sacred ministers duly ordained after sufficient instruction and formation, may exercise the office of "teaching, sanctifying and governing". The lay faithful may, with a canonical mission from the Bishop, perform an ancillary ecclesial ministry of handing on the faith.

In recent years, for various reasons, you, may Brother Bishops, have encountered difficulties, since persons who are not "ordained", and sometimes not even baptized, control and take decisions concerning important ecclesial questions, including the appointment of Bishops, in the name of various State agencies. Consequently, we have witnessed a demeaning of the Petrine and Episcopal ministries by virtue of a vision of the Church according to which the Supreme Pontiff, the Bishops and the priests risk becoming de facto persons without office and without power. Yet in fact, as stated earlier, the Petrine and Episcopal ministries are essential and integral elements of Catholic doctrine on the sacramental structure of the Church. The nature of the Church is a gift of the Lord Jesus, because "his gifts were that some should be apostles, some prophets, some evangelists, some pastors and teachers, to equip the saints for the work of ministry, for building up the body of Christ, until we all attain to the unity of the faith and of the knowledge of the Son of God, to mature manhood, to the measure of the stature of the fullness of Christ" (Eph 4:11-13).

Communion and unity – let me repeat (cf. section 5 above)... are essential elements of the Catholic Church: therefore the proposal for a Church that is "independent" of the Holy See, in the religious sphere, is incompatible with Catholic doctrine.

I am aware of the grave difficulties which you have to address in the aforementioned situation in order to remain faithful to Christ, to his Church and to the Successor of Peter. Reminding you that – as Saint Paul said (cf. Rom 8:35-39) – no difficulty can separate us from the love of Christ, I am confident that you will do everything possible, trusting in the Lord's grace, to safeguard unity and ecclesial communion even at the cost of great sacrifices.

Many members of the Chinese episcopate who have guided the Church in recent decades have offered and continue to offer a shining testimony to their own communities and to be universal Church. Once again, let a heartfelt hymn of praise and thanksgiving be sung to the "chief Shepherd" of the flock (1 Pet 5:4): in fact, it must not be forgotten that many Bishops have undergone persecution and have been impeded in the exercise of the ministry, and some of them have made the Church fruitful with the shedding of their blood. Modern times and the consequent challenge of the new evangelization highlight the role of the Episcopal ministry. As John Paul II said to the Pastors from every part of the world who gathered in Rome for the celebration of the Jubilee, "the Pastor is the first to take responsibility for and to encourage the ecclesial community, both in the requirement of communion and in the missionary outreach. Regarding the relativism and subjectivism which mar so much of contemporary culture, Bishops are called to defend and promote the doctrinal unity of their faithful. Concerned for every situation in which the faith has been lost or is unknown, they work with all their strength for evangelization, preparing priests, religious and lay people for this task and making the necessary resources available".

On the same occasion, my venerable predecessor recalled that "the Bishop, a successor of the Apostles, is someone for whom Christ is everything: 'For to me to live is Christ...' (Phil 1:21). He must bear witness to this in all his actions. The Second Vatican Council teaches: 'Bishops should devote themselves to their apostolic office as witnesses of Christ to all' (Decree Christus Dominus, 11)"

Concerning Episcopal service, then, I take the opportunity to recall something I said recently: "The Bishops are primarily responsible for building up the Church as a family of God and a place of mutual help and availability. To be able to carry out this mission, you received with Episcopal consecration three special offices: the *munus docendi, the munus sanctificandi and the munus regendi*, which all together constitute the *munus pascendi*. In particular, the aim of the munus regendi is growth in ecclesial communion, that is, in building a community in agreement and listening to the Apostles' teaching, the breaking of bread, prayer and fellowship. Closely linked to the offices of teaching and of sanctifying, that of governing – the *munus regendi* precisely – constitutes for the Bishop an authentic act of love for God and for one's neighbor, which is expressed in pastoral charity."

As in the rest of the world, in China too the Church is governed by Bishops who, through Episcopal ordination conferred upon them by other validly ordained Bishops, have received, together with the sanctifying office, the offices of teaching and governing the people entrusted to them in their respective particular Churches, with a power that is conferred by God through the graces of the sacrament of Holy Orders. The offices of teaching and governing "however, by their very nature can be exercised only in hierarchical communion with the head and members of the college" of Bishops. In fact, as the Council went on to say, "a person is made a member of the episcopal body in virtue of the sacramental consecration and by hierarchical communion with the head and members of the college."

Currently, all the Bishops of the Catholic Church in China are sons of the Chinese People. Notwithstanding many grave difficulties, the Catholic Church in China, by a particular grace of the Holy Spirit, has never been deprived of the ministry of legitimate Pastors who have preserved the apostolic succession intact. We must thank the Lord for this constant presence, not without suffering, of Bishops who have received episcopal ordination in conformity with Catholic tradition, that is to say, in communion with the Bishop of Rome, Successor of Peter, and at the hands of validly and legitimately ordained Bishops in observance of the rite of the Catholic Church.

Some of them, not wishing to be subjected to undue control exercised over the life of the Church, and eager to maintain total fidelity to the Successor Peter and to Catholic doctrine, have felt themselves constrained to opt for clandestine consecration. The clandestine condition is not a normal feature of the Church's life, and history shows that Pastors and faithful have recourse to it only amid suffering, in the desire to maintain the integrity of their faith and to resist interference from State agencies in matters pertaining intimately to the Church's life. For this reason the Holy See hopes that these legitimate Pastors may be recognized as such by governmental authorities for civil effects too – insofar as these are necessary – and that all the faithful may be able to express their faith freely in the social context in which they live.

Other Pastors, however, under the pressure of particular circumstances, have consented to receive episcopal ordination without the pontifical mandate, but have subsequently asked to be received into communion with the Successor of Peter and with their other brothers in the episcopate. The Pope, considering the sincerity of their sentiments and the complexity of the situation, and taking into account the opinion of neighboring bishops, by virtue of his proper responsibility as universal Pastor of the Church, has granted them the full and legitimate exercise of episcopal jurisdiction. This initiative of the Pope resulted from knowledge of the particular circumstances of their ordination and from his profound pastoral concern to favour the reestablishment of full communion. Unfortunately, in most cases, priests and the faithful have not been adequately informed that their Bishop has been legitimized, and this has given rise to a number of grave problems of conscience. What is more, some legitimized Bishops have failed to provide any clear signs to prove that they have been legitimized. For this reason it is indispensable, for the spiritual good of the diocesan communities concerned, that legitimation, once it has occurred, is brought into the public domain at the earliest opportunity, and that the legitimized Bishops provide unequivocal and increasing signs of full communion with the Successor of Peter.

Finally, there are certain Bishops – a very small number of them – who have been ordained without the Pontifical mandate and who have not asked for or have not yet obtained the necessary legitimation. According to the doctrine of the Catholic Church, they are to be considered illegitimate, but validly ordained, as long as it is certain that they have received ordination from validly ordained bishops and that the Catholic rite of episcopal ordination has been respected. Therefore, although not in communion with the Pope, they exercise their ministry validly in the administration of the sacraments, even if they do so illegitimately. What great spiritual enrichment would ensure for the Church in China if, the necessary conditions having been established, these Pastors too were to enter into communion with the Successor of Peter and with the entire Catholic episcopate! Not only would their episcopal ministry be legitimized, there would also be an enrichment of their communion with the priests and the faithful who consider the Church in China part of the Catholic Church, united with the Bishop of Rome and with all the other particular Churches spread throughout the world.

In individual nations, all the legitimate Bishops constitute an Episcopal Conference, governed according to its own statutes, which by the norms of canon law must be approved by the Apostolic See. Such an Episcopal Conference expresses the fraternal communion of all the Bishops of a nation and treats the doctrinal and pastoral questions that are significant for the entire Catholic community of the country without, however, interfering the exercise of the ordinary and immediate power of each Bishop in his own diocese. Moreover, every Episcopal Conference maintains opportune and useful contacts with the civil authorities of the place, partly in order to favor cooperation between the Church and the State, but it is obvious that an Episcopal Conference cannot be subjected to any civil authority in questions of faith and of living according to the faith (*fides et mores*, sacramental life), which are exclusively the competence of the Church.

In the light of the principles expounded above, the present College of Catholic Bishops of China cannot be recognized as an Episcopal Conference by the Apostolic See: the "clandestine" Bishops, those not recognized by the Government but in communion with the Pope, are not part of it; it includes Bishops who are still illegitimate, and it is governed by statues that contain elements incompatible with Catholic doctrine.

Appointment of Bishops

9. As all of you know, one of the most delicate problems in relations between the Holy See and the authorities of your country is the question of episcopal appointments. On the one hand, it is understandable that governmental authorities are attentive to the choice of those who will carry out the important role of the leading and shepherding the local Catholic communities, given the social implications which – in China as in the rest of the world – this function has in the civil sphere as well as the spiritual. On the other hand, the Holy See follows the appointment of Bishops with special care since this touches the very heart of the life of the Church, inasmuch as the appointment of Bishops by the Pope is the guarantee of the unity of the Church and of hierarchical communion. For this reason the Code of Canon Law (cf. c. 1382) lays down grave sanctions both for the Bishop who freely confers episcopal ordination without an apostolic mandate and for the one who receives it: such an ordination in fact inflicts a painful would upon ecclesial communion and constitutes a grave violation of canonical disciple.

The Pope, when he issues the apostolic mandate for the ordination of a Bishop, exercises his supreme spiritual authority: this authority and this intervention remain within the strictly religious sphere. It is not, therefore, a question of a political authority, unduly asserting itself in the internal affairs of a State and offending against its sovereignty.

The appointment of Bishops for a particular religious community is understood, also in international documents, as a constitutive element of the full exercise of the right to religious freedom. The Holy See would love to be completely free to appoint Bishops; therefore, considering the recent particular developments of the Church in China, I trust that an accord can be reached with the Government so as to resolve certain questions regarding the choice of candidates for the episcopate, the publication of the appointment of Bishops, and the recognition – concerning civil effects where necessary – of the new Bishops on the part of the civil authorities.

Finally, as to the choice of candidates for the episcopate, while knowing your difficulties in this regard, I would like to remind you that they should be worthy priests, respected and loved by the faithful, models of life in the faith, and that they should possess a certain experience in the pastoral ministry, so that they are equipped to address the burdensome responsibility of a Pastor of the Church. Whenever it proves impossible within a diocese to find suitable candidates to occupy the episcopal see, the cooperation of Bishops in neighboring dioceses can help to identify suitable candidates.

LaVergne, TN USA
17 November 2009
164455LV00002B/1/P